Rocky Sung's Guide to
Chinese Astrology and Feng Shui

The Year of the Horse

2002

Rocky Sung

Thorsons

Thorsons
An Imprint of HarperCollins*Publishers*
77–85 Fulham Palace Road
Hammersmith, London W6 8JB

The Thorsons website address is:
www.thorsons.com

Thorsons is a trademark of
HarperCollins*Publishers*
Published by Thorsons 2001

1 3 5 7 9 10 8 6 4 2

A catalogue record for this book
is available from the British Library

ISBN 0 00 712412 0

Printed in Great Britain by
Omnia Books Ltd, Glasgow

Contents

Rocky Sung is a respected authority on Feng Shui, highly commendable for his honesty, directness and professionalism. He studies all factors involved and considers all available resources before making any recommendations. He does not propose major changes that will waste current resources, but rather suggests improvements that will maximize their full Feng Shui potential. His expertise and improvements have induced a more positive relationship between man and his environment.

Andre G. Rolli, General Manager,
Westin Hotel, Shanghai

About the Author

Sung Siu-Kwong, hereafter referred to as Rocky Sung, is instantly recognizable by the international Chinese community as the top Feng Shui Master of what must surely be the Feng Shui capital of the world – Hong Kong.

His many best-selling Chinese books on Feng Shui, a successful Feng Shui television programme viewed by Chinese communities across the globe, countless interviews on international television shows (such as on CNN), press and magazine interviews conducted in many languages, plus his reputation as a scrupulous results-driven consultant, have assured him this international recognition.

Born in China, Sung grew up in Hong Kong. He graduated from Taiwan University with a degree in history, and went on to obtain his Master's Degree from the University of Illinois. His interest in Feng Shui dates back to his schooldays, when his love of hiking found him out on the rigorous mountain trails of the territory. It was on these outdoor expeditions that an elderly Master taught him how to locate the 'veins of the dragon' – the flow of the mountain. As his knowledge of Chinese history grew, so too did his knowledge of this ancient Chinese tradition.

Sung has millions of followers and an enviable multinational blue-chip client list that includes the Swire Group of Companies and the Westin International Hotel Group.

Westerners in Hong Kong have long followed the beliefs of their Chinese counterparts; now, as the entire Western world expresses an interest in Eastern philosophies and traditions, the name Rocky Sung has become increasingly synonymous with the art of Feng Shui throughout the world.

He has offices in Hong Kong and Los Angeles, and family contacts in New York.

Introduction

T his book is unique and outstanding because it consists of the
following four key factors which distinguish it from all other
books about Chinese Horoscope:

1 The application of the traditional Stars in the Chinese Horoscope into
   the calculation of the fate of different Signs.
2 The use of proverbs to indicate the fate of a Sign for a particular
   month.
3 The application of Feng Shui to improve the fortune of different Signs.
4 An easy-to-read chart to remind readers of how to 'do the right things
   at the right time every day' in 2002 (the Day-by-day Analysis of Luck).

Application of Traditional Stars of the Chinese Horoscope

This is the first book in English which uses a pure Chinese
Horoscope methodology to predict the future. It is not at all
influenced by Western Astrology. Chinese traditional Astrology is
completely different to Western Astrology.

The Chinese method of predicting the future was developed

some 2,000 years ago, and is calculated according to the distribution of Stars within a specific Sign. The number of Lucky and Unlucky Stars within a Sign determines a person's fate for the year. The distribution varies on a year-to-year basis for each Sign, therefore the fate of each Sign changes annually.

This calculating system has been practised in China for centuries and has proved to be quite effective. I have applied this system in the writing of my Chinese-language yearly fortune books, which have sold in large numbers since 1985.

The Lucky and Unlucky Stars of the Chinese Horoscope have a very long history. Giving the history of Chinese predictions without applying the traditional method, as is so often seen in Western books on Chinese Astrology, is definitely incorrect. Unfortunately a lot of so-called 'Chinese Horoscope' books in print are therefore inaccurate.

I have no bias against Western or Indian Astrology – quite the contrary, I have a deep and sincere respect for them. However, a mixture of Chinese and Western Astrology diminishes the substance and destroys the basic nature of both.

Considering that most non-Chinese readers have no knowledge of the Stars that influence the Chinese Astrological predictions, I have explained the origins, meaning and modern implications of each one. After reading the Stars, both Lucky and Unlucky, which apply to your Sign for the forthcoming year, you will have a clear picture of your fate.

This book provides the reader with predictions for the entire year, with daily reference charts for every day of the year in the Chinese Calendar (see pages 228–333).

The monthly prognosis is meant to prepare the reader on how to face each month. It will give you the opportunity to protect yourself when facing bad luck, and it will give you the opportunity to activate initiatives when you know you are heading for good luck.

The 12 Chinese Horoscope Signs

The Horse
The Sheep (Goat)
The Monkey
The Rooster
The Dog
The Pig
The Mouse (Rat)
The Ox
The Tiger
The Rabbit
The Dragon
The Snake

Individuals are classified according to their birth date. The chart on page xiii will allow readers to check which is their Sign.

Snake	Horse	Sheep	Monkey
Dragon			Rooster
Rabbit			Dog
Tiger	Ox	Mouse	Pig

The 12 Signs are divided into 12 squares, as shown above. The distribution of the Stars, both Lucky and Unlucky, within the squares will determine the fate of each of the 12 Signs for the year ahead.

The Stars are not evenly distributed; this makes a difference. Each Star is listed individually so that the reader has a clear picture of his or her fortune. Those Signs with more Lucky Stars will have a good year, while those with more Unlucky Stars will have a rough, even a poor, year. There are 20 Lucky Stars and 46 Unlucky Stars mentioned in this book.

Proverbs and Fortune

Each chapter for a particular Sign has a General Overview of the Year for 2002, followed by Monthly In-depth Forecasts. Each of these monthly sections begins with a proverb, to enable readers to know at a glance precisely what challenges they are going to face in a given month.

Proverbs are derived from the experiences of daily life. Therefore, after very careful consideration I have decided upon an appropriate proverb to summarize the monthly fortune for each Sign. Through this I hope that readers will have a much better understanding of their fortune for each month.

I sincerely hope that this method of my own will benefit readers throughout the world.

Using Feng Shui

The main Feng Shui tactics are discussed at the end of the monthly forecasts of each sign, as a suggestion for improving fortune practically and effectively. Each outlines the Feng Shui directions, colours, lucky numbers and lucky charms for each Sign.

These Feng Shui tactics are practical and effective in improving the fortune of every sign. They are based on combining the calculation of the Five Elements, the Yin and Yang, and the distribution of Lucky and Unlucky Stars throughout the year.

Just as different kinds of medicine will suit different people, different Feng Shui tactics will suit different Signs. To avoid taking the wrong 'medicine', readers should therefore not try to apply the Feng Shui recommended for any Sign but their own.

Day-by-day Analysis of Luck

From the experiences of their daily lives through numerous generations, the ancient Chinese found that certain activities would meet with much greater success if undertaken on certain days. Along the same lines, certain things can go wrong if attempted on the wrong day. Thus the ancient Chinese realized that there was a close correlation between human activities and certain days. Consequently, the concept of 'doing the right thing at the right time every day' has been deeply ingrained into the Chinese psyche and society for centuries.

The Day-by-day Analysis of Luck tables will prove helpful in improving one's overall fortune. The same charts have appeared in my Chinese-language books, and have proven useful to my readers over the past 16 years.

The charts begin at 30 December 2001 and end at 31 December 2002. Beneath the charts there are brief forecasts for the Signs, to help readers know what they are going to face during that particular period of time. This is meant as a helpful supplement to the Monthly In-depth Forecasts for the Signs in the previous chapters.

According to the Chinese calendar commonly used, the year of the Horse begins on 12 February 2002 and ends on 31 January 2003 of the Western calendar. But the Chinese traditional Astrology has different ideas about the division of the year. The 'Lap Chung Day' 立春日 – that is, the 'Day of the Beginning of Spring', is used as a division line of the year. Consequently, the year of Horse begins on 4 February 2002 and ends on 3 February 2003 according to traditional Chinese Astrology. As a writer of fortune books for more than 16 years, I am sure that the calculation of fate for the 12 signs within the year is made more accurate by using this traditional system.

How to Establish Your Chinese Sign

1905 – Snake	1906 – Horse **	1907 – Sheep **	1908 – Monkey **
1909 – Rooster	1910 – Dog **	1911 – Pig **	1912 – Mouse **
1913 – Ox	1914 – Tiger	1915 – Rabbit **	1916 – Dragon **
1917 – Snake	1918 – Horse	1919 – Sheep **	1920 – Monkey **
1921 – Rooster	1922 – Dog	1923 – Pig **	1924 – Mouse **
1925 – Ox	1926 – Tiger	1927 – Rabbit **	1928 – Dragon **
1929 – Snake	1930 – Horse	1931 – Sheep **	1932 – Monkey **
1933 – Rooster	1934 – Dog	1935 – Pig **	1936 – Mouse **
1937 – Ox	1938 – Tiger	1939 – Rabbit **	1940 – Dragon **
1941 – Snake	1942 – Horse	1943 – Sheep **	1944 – Monkey **
1945 – Rooster	1946 – Dog	1947 – Pig	1948 – Mouse **
1949 – Ox	1950 – Tiger	1951 – Rabbit	1952 – Dragon **
1953 – Snake	1954 – Horse	1955 – Sheep	1956 – Monkey **
1957 – Rooster	1958 – Dog	1959 – Pig	1960 – Mouse **
1961 – Ox	1962 – Tiger	1963 – Rabbit	1964 – Dragon **
1965 – Snake	1966 – Horse	1967 – Sheep	1968 – Monkey **
1969 – Rooster	1970 – Dog	1971 – Pig	1972 – Mouse **
1973 – Ox	1974 – Tiger	1975 – Rabbit	1976 – Dragon **
1977 – Snake	1978 – Horse	1979 – Sheep	1980 – Monkey **
1981 – Rooster	1982 – Dog	1983 – Pig	1984 – Mouse
1985 – Ox	1986 – Tiger	1987 – Rabbit	1988 – Dragon
1989 – Snake	1990 – Horse	1991 – Sheep	1992 – Monkey
1993 – Rooster	1994 – Dog	1995 – Pig	1996 – Mouse
1997 – Ox	1998 – Tiger	1999 – Rabbit	2000 – Dragon
2001 – Snake	2002 – Horse	2003 – Sheep	2004 – Monkey

According to the Chinese Horoscope, people are classified into a certain Sign according to their birth year. This chart will help you to establish your exact Sign. Please refer to the first page of each Sign for more detailed information.

There is a difference in year division between the Chinese Calendar and the Western Calendar. 4 February of the Western Calendar is the dividing line. For example, if a person was born on 3 February 1998, then he or she is considered to be an Ox. But if a person was born on 5 February 1998, then he or she is considered to be a Tiger.

Occasionally this dividing line changes to 5 February. This will call for a slight adjustment. These exceptional years are indicated on the chart by **.

Chapter One

The

Horse

Years of the Horse

1918 (4/Feb/18—4/Feb/19) 1966 (4/Feb/66—3/Feb/67)
1930 (4/Feb/30—4/Feb/31) 1978 (4/Feb/78—3/Feb/79)
1942 (4/Feb/42—4/Feb/43) 1990 (4/Feb/90—3/Feb/91)
1954 (4/Feb/54—3/Feb/55) 2002 (4/Feb/02—4/Feb/03)

If you have any doubt about the classification of the 12 animal signs, or the divisions of months and years, please refer to pages xiii–xiv.

Distribution of the Stars within the Sign for 2002

Lucky Star   **Unlucky Stars**

The Star of Commander   Sword's Edge
                        Watch-dog of the Year
                        Lying Corpse

Lucky Star
The Star of Commander

Although the ancient Chinese loved peace, they also respected their local military commander, who was there to protect them from foreign enemies. A courageous and responsible commander signified a guardian of the peace and protection from suffering.

The appearance of this Star is a very good omen. It will not only enrich a Sign's luck, but will also minimize negative influences from Unlucky Stars.

Unlucky Stars
Sword's Edge

Swords and knives were not favoured by the peace-loving ancient Chinese. People would easily be hurt by the sharp edges of these dangerous weapons.

Consequently, the 'Sword's Edge' Star is considered to be a bad omen, calling for precautionary measures regarding your personal safety. This is especially relevant when engaging in outdoor activities and handling sharp objects.

Watch-dog of the Year

In Chinese mythology, a very fierce animal called 'Year' went about swallowing people just as a New Year was ushered in. To protect themselves, the ancient Chinese used firecrackers to scare it away. Over time this fierce animal would be tamed, to become the Watchdog of the Year among the Chinese folk. Still, it could be quite dangerous if irritated.

When this Star appears it is best to behave, keep a low profile and take care not to offend anyone. To avoid problems, keep in mind the phrase 'Let sleeping dogs lie'.

In ancient China, to die peacefully at home was considered to be a blessing. In contrast, to die in an accident in the street or some other public place was considered the worst thing that could happen. Such unexpected and 'poorly timed' deaths were considered to be a kind of divine retribution for a person's bad deeds.

When this Star appears, be very careful not to commit any wrong-doings, and at the same time pay special attention to safety when engaged in outdoor activities.

General Overview of the Year

Because of the appearance of the Unlucky Star 'Watchdog of the Year' within their sign, Horses will have numerous disputes and conflicts both in their business and private life this year. Unless they can settle these matters properly, Horses will not be able to have a successful and peaceful year in 2002.

First of all, Horses should try their best to identify hidden enemies to avoid a possible sudden attack from behind. Then they should try to improve their business relationships as much as possible. Horses will be more productive if they can create a harmonious working atmosphere for themselves at this stage.

The appearance of the 'Sword's Edge' Star indicates that Horses should try to keep a low profile and never try to offend or provoke their superiors. Otherwise, their jobs will be seriously jeopardized as a consequence. Fortunately, Horses will be able to overcome most of the difficulties and challenges at work during the year because of the appearance of the Lucky Star 'The Star of Commander' within their sign.

The fortune of Horses in money affairs is satisfactory – not too good, but not too bad either. Their regular income will be quite steady, and their investments will bring some profits to them, so that Horses will have not too much to worry about financially. However, their extravagant expenses will become the main source of their sorrows this year. Horses must try to do something about this before it gets out of control.

Horses must watch out for their health and safety very carefully this year, or they will be very sorry. It's necessary for Horses to keep away from sharp objects such as swords, knives, daggers, saws, spears and so on, to avoid a serious injury.

This won't be a very romantic year for Horses. If they are looking for a marriage this year, Horses will be deeply disappointed. They will be quite emotional and sensitive about their love affairs. It's necessary for Horses to control their temper to avoid serious conflicts with their lovers and friends.

Fortunately, their romantic life will turn to a new page at year end.

Career	* * *
Money	* *
Health	*
Love	*

* * * = Pretty Good/* * = Fair/* = Unsatisfactory

Career * * *

Although Horses will have a lot of disputes and conflicts at work this year, they will be quite productive if they can handle these matters properly before they get out of control. How to improve their business relationships with their colleagues and clients will be the major concern of Horses throughout the year. It would be much better if Horses can keep a low profile to get rid of jealousy among their colleagues and avoid offending their superiors.

Fortunately, Horses will be able to overcome most of their difficulties and challenges this year with the help of the Lucky Star 'The Star of Commander'. Horses will have better luck in business during the first, third, sixth and tenth months. However, they must try to keep a low profile and struggle very hard for their survival during the second, fifth, seventh, eighth, ninth and the last two months of the year.

Money **

This won't be a very profitable year for Horses, but it won't be too bad, either. They will have a stable and satisfactory regular income throughout the year, but they can hardly expect to have extra income from taking part in lotteries or gambling. What they have to watch carefully is their expenses. Unless they can keep to a tight budget, their expenses will get out of control without any warning and that would definitely bring about very terrible consequences for their financial situation. Horses must pay special attention to their money affairs during the second, third, fifth, eighth, ninth and last months of the year.

Health *

Because of the appearance of the Unlucky Star 'Sword's Edge' within their sign, Horses will be easily injured by sharp objects accidentally. Thus it will be necessary for Horses to keep away from those dangerous swords, knives, saws and so on to ensure their personal safety. Fortunately, Horses will be quite healthy this year, but they must try to keep away from drugs and alcohol, or their health will be seriously spoiled. Horses must watch out for their road safety during the fourth month, and they should try to get as much rest and sleep as possible to relax themselves during the fifth and seventh months.

Love *

It won't be easy for Horses to be appreciated by the opposite sex this year. That means, this won't be a romantic year for Horses, and they will be deeply disappointed if they are looking for an unforgettable romance or a happy marriage. Unless Horses can control their emotions in their private lives, they will scare their lovers and friends away from them. However, Horses will have better luck in love affairs during the first, fourth and sixth months.

Monthly In-depth Forecasts
The First Month (4 February – 5 March)

Make hay while the sun shines

Horses will have a pretty good start to the beginning of the year. There will be several opportunities knocking on their doors during this period of time. Horses should not be too hesitant, because time and tide wait for no man. In other words, Horses should try to make hay while the sun shines. On the other hand, it would be a total waste of time and effort if they try to make hay on rainy days. Horses will be quite creative and productive this month, so that they will make important achievements at work so long as they are not just fooling around. If they wish to carry out their new projects or to change jobs, this month will be a very good time to do so. Horses will become quite persuasive this month, and they will be very successful if they can make good use of their talents.

The fortune in money affairs will be quite good for Horses. They will be able to gain profits from different kinds of investments and projects. It's a good time for Horses to buy properties and valuable items. Although they will have luck in gambling, Horses should be more cautious about this towards the end of the month.

This will be a romantic month for Horses. However, they should try to be honest to their lovers, because any cheating in love affairs will never fly during this period.

The Second Month (6 March – 4 April)

Curiosity killed the cat

All of a sudden, bad luck will come swiftly this month, so that Horses must keep their eyes wide open to watch out for possible dangers. They will have a better chance of survival at work if they know how to protect themselves at this critical moment. That means if Horses can keep a low profile and keep their wits about them in order to keep away from danger, they will survive under heavy pressure. Otherwise, they would become an easy target for their competitors. Horses must curb their curiosity, because 'curiosity killed the cat'.

This month is definitely not a good time for Horses to start a new project, or to change to a new job. Most important of all, Horses should never try to provoke or offend their superiors at this critical moment.

Because the fortune of Horses in money affairs drops down sharply this month, this is definitely not a profitable month for them. It would be much better if Horses stop trying their luck in high-risk investments and gambling.

Horses must mind what they say at social gatherings this month. Otherwise they will be in deep trouble in the months to come. Besides that, Horses should try to communicate more with their family members to clear up unnecessary misunderstandings. It's worthwhile to do so, and they should not hesitate.

The Third Month (5 April – 5 May)

There's no such thing as a free lunch

Horses have to work very hard for themselves if they want to see breakthroughs at work this month. No one will provide the necessary help to them in their business but themselves. That means, there's no free lunch – if Horses want benefits, they'll have to pay for them themselves during this period.

Along with their diligence, Horses should have more enthusiasm at work, otherwise their success will be much diminished. It's very important for Horses to keep their mouths shut and talk nothing about their colleagues if they don't want to have endless troubles in the following months. Horses have to make several important decisions and to take several calculated risks in business during this period of time. Otherwise they will miss good opportunities and will be therefore left far behind their competitors.

This is absolutely not a romantic month for Horses. They will be somewhat isolated by their close friends or lovers during this period. It's very important for Horses to find out who their real friends are, and who their real enemies are. They will be in big trouble in both their private and business life if they fail to do so.

If possible, Horses should try not to ask for any loans this month. And they must try to pay up their bills as soon as possible. 'Out of debt, out of trouble,' – this will be especially true this month.

The Fourth Month (6 May – 5 June)

Fine feathers make fine birds

Horses should try to dress themselves up this month, because their appearance will play a very important role in their success, in both their business and private life, during this period. This will be a bargaining and negotiating month for Horses, and their nice and proper appearance will help them quite a lot in handling these matters. Otherwise, they will be easily beaten by their opponents. Horses should keep in mind that proper dress is much better than loud or excessive clothing, and sincere speech is much better than flattery when bargaining and negotiating. Besides that, Horses should try to find good partners and form an alliance with them if they want to see splendid achievements this year. Otherwise, Horses will be easily defeated if they try to fight their way all alone.

Horses will have much better luck in love affairs this month if they dress themselves up properly. They will get a nice surprise if they send gifts or love letters to their loved one during this period.

Horses will be in good health and in high spirits this month, but they must try to keep away from alcohol and drugs, or their health will be badly damaged. They must try to mind their road safety near the end of the month.

The Fifth Month (6 June – 6 July)

You don't miss the water til the well runs dry

This month is definitely not a profitable period of time for Horses, so they must try to keep to a very tight budget and try to watch out for any leaks in their accounting systems. Otherwise, Horses will lose a lot of money and easily get into financial problems. They must try to curb their extravagant habits and save as much money as they can, or they will run out of money sooner or later. Horses must try not be too greedy, and should be more cautious in handling their investments. Gambling at this critical moment would be suicide.

There will be numerous personal disputes at work this month. It's necessary for Horses to settle these peacefully and patiently as soon as possible. As a matter of fact, Horses would be in a much better situation if they can improve their relationships with the people working around them during this period.

Horses must try to get enough rest and sleep, to avoid total exhaustion. Their health will be in deep trouble if they don't take care of themselves properly. They should keep in mind that prevention is much better than cure.

The Sixth Month (7 July – 7 August)

Divide and conquer

Because of the appearance of several Lucky Stars within the Sign this month, the luck of Horses will be much improved. This will be most obvious in their business lives. Obstacles and personal disputes at work will disappear one after the other during this period, so that it would be a very good time for Horses to carry out their new projects. However, they should understand the art of 'Divide and conquer.' That means Horses have to try to separate their opponents one by one, and then use different tactics to deal with them accordingly. Horses should try their best to prevent their opponents from joining together, or they will be in a very difficult situation in the months to come.

Horses should try to diversify their investments this month, and try not to put all their eggs in one basket. Fortunately, Horses will have luck in lotteries and gambling.

This will be a romantic month for Horses, and they will be quite popular with the opposite sex. One thing they should keep in mind is that they must keep a low profile in love affairs, and try not to show off too much, or there will be endless troubles waiting for them.

The Seventh Month (8 August – 7 September)

Do as you would be done by

Horses should keep a low profile and try to concentrate on their own work this month. Horses should be honest and polite to those who are working around them, so they can win respect and support from them in return. They will be in trouble if they turn a cold shoulder to their colleagues and subordinates. In conclusion, Horses must maintain a pleasant manner at work during this period. This month would not be a good time for Horses to start any new projects, especially near the end of the month, because they would have to face different kinds of obstacles right from the beginning.

The health of Horses will be endangered by infections, so that they must watch their personal hygiene this month. They should also stay away from crowded and dirty places. At the beginning of the month, Horses should try to keep their eyes wide open to watch out for their home safety.

Horses should be more considerate to the other people in their private life, or they will be isolated. Better communication and better mutual understanding are the most effective remedies for their love relationships and friendships this month.

The Eighth Month (8 September – 7 October)

Cross that bridge when you come to it

It is very important for Horses to stay fixed on their own work responsibilities this month, or their jobs will be seriously endangered. This month is definitely not a favourable period of time to make any important change at work, because the Horse's weaknesses will be exposed to their opponents by doing so. Horses should understand that everything takes time, and they have to wait for a better moment if they wish to reform their careers. In other words, Horses must keep in mind that they should 'cross that bridge when they get to it'. They should not take any unnecessary risks at this critical moment.

Because their fortune in money affairs will fluctuate from time to time this month, Horses must not try to risk their money in investments or gambling. If they were to do so, their income might be jeopardized during this period of time.

Horses will become quite emotional this month in their private life. They must try to keep calm in their love affairs. It's necessary for them to walk away for a while if they find that they are in danger of losing their temper in front of their lovers.

The Ninth Month (8 October – 6 November)

Big fish eat little fish

Horses have to try to use their wits to protect themselves from being swallowed up by their powerful opponents this month. This month will be a critical moment for their survival at work. All their previous efforts will have been totally wasted if they fail to protect themselves from being engulfed in the cruel business world. Big fish eat little fish – a common phenomenon in the business world. Horses must try to keep alert and stay away from those dangerous big fish. Forming alliances with others will be a big help to their survival, so Horses should think about this carefully.

It's necessary for Horses to take good care of their money at this critical moment. They should not let the 'Big fish eat little fish' scenario happen to them in financial affairs. There may be somebody trying to take their financial rewards away from them by means of dirty tricks within this period of time.

Horses will be bothered very much by gossips in their private life this month. The best way forward is try to keep their mouths shut, and walk away from those talkative people.

The Tenth Month (7 November – 6 December)

After a storm comes calm

All of a sudden, the business troubles of last month will disappear during this period. Horses will be able to enjoy themselves in a much more relaxed working atmosphere this month. It's time for them to think about their future business developments, but they should not take action for the time being. Horses will be quite successful in their career if they can identify their weaknesses and try to do something about them at this stage. They should keep in mind that co-operation will bring more profits than stiff competition. That means Horses should try to persuade their competitors to reach a compromise rather than to fight each other. Horses will be very productive in the months to come if they can improve their personal and business relationships within this period.

This will be a profitable month for Horses. Their investments will bring handsome shares to them. Besides that, they will have extra income from different sources.

Horses will be in pretty good health this month. But they should try to relax and take a break or holiday to refresh themselves. They will probably have a very good chance to meet someone attractive while travelling.

The Eleventh Month (7 December – 5 January)

Ask no questions and hear no lies

This will be one of the most unfavourable months of the year for Horses, so they should be more conservative in handling their business. They should keep a low profile in and out of the office and they must try to concentrate on their own work and ask no questions about other people's business. This will save Horses from endless trouble. There will be numerous drastic changes in their working areas, so that Horses must try to adapt themselves to the new circumstances without asking silly questions. They will have a better chance of survival by doing so. There will be rumours and gossip at work – Horses should listen but say nothing.

Apart from this, Horses must keep alert during this period so that they are not cheated by liars. Otherwise they will suffer a big loss in business and financial affairs.

There will probably be problems between Horses and their lovers this month. They will face a broken relationship if they fail to reach a mutual understanding with their lovers. The best way to save their relationship at this critical moment is to try not to criticize their lovers and forget about the rumours about them.

The Twelfth Month (6 January – 3 February)

The road to hell is paved with good intentions

Although the luck of Horses will see some improvement this month, there still will be numerous obstacles in their business lives. Therefore, Horses should think carefully before they take action during this period of time, or they will meet with a sudden big fall in the last month of the year. Horses must consider the whole situation from different angles carefully before they come up with any conclusions. Otherwise, their good intentions may bring destructive results. If they want to help people, Horses must make sure they're not over-extending themselves or going beyond their abilities as they try to reach out a helping hand. Worst of all, their good intentions might be misunderstood by some other people, and this would bring them endless trouble.

Horses will be busily engaged in different social gatherings this month. Although they will be quite popular at parties, unfortunately they won't have too much luck in love affairs. Horses must watch their diet, and try to avoid over-drinking during this period.

Because their fortune in money affairs will be going up and down like a roller-coaster this month, Horses must forget about investments and gambling at this critical moment or they will lose more than they ever anticipated. It's better for Horses to save their money for the coming rainy days.

Using Feng Shui to Improve Fortune: Directions, Colours, Numbers and Lucky Charm

The ancient Chinese used the traditional Horoscope to predict their fortune on a yearly basis – they used the art of Feng Shui to improve their luck.

It was their belief that the application of tactical Feng Shui would change their bad luck into good, and make their good luck improve even more.

This same method is still effective in today's modern world.

There are four main elements which I will use in tactical Feng Shui:

- Lucky Directions
- Lucky Colours
- Lucky Numbers
- Lucky Charm

Horses will face numerous conflicts and disputes, in both their business and private lives this year. They must try to pay more attention to taking care of these matters, or they will mess up the whole thing and become a sure loser at year end. However, if they can improve their business and personal relationships, Horses will be quite productive and happy throughout the year. Horses should try to keep a low profile and try not to offend or provoke their superiors, or their jobs might be jeopardized. The fortune of Horses will be satisfactory overall – neither too good nor too bad.

What Horses have to worry about is not their income but their expenses. The health of Horses will be not so good this year, so it's necessary for them to mind their health and safety closely, or they will be very sorry. In love affairs, Horses won't have too much luck. If they are looking for true love this year, they will be deeply disappointed. Fortunately, their romantic life will turn over a new leaf at year end.

I would suggest applying the following Feng Shui tactics to improve luck so that Horses don't have to worry too much about their fate within the year.

Lucky Directions

The most favourable directions of the year for Horses are **Southeast**, **Southwest** and **Northeast**. Horses should sleep or sit in these directions if they wish to improve their fortune.

To make this procedure very simple, divide the house or room into nine imaginary squares. Then, using a compass, check the exact direction of each square as shown in Figure 1. This will help to ensure that you do not make a mistake with the direction.

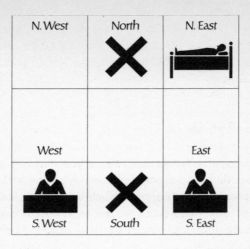

N. West	North	N. East
	✕	🛏
West		East
🧑 S. West	✕ South	🧑 S. East

Figure 1

Horses should sit in the Southeast or Southwest at work or while studying; this will ensure that their achievements are much greater than the Stars intended. To improve health and achieve a good night's sleep, Horses should position the bed in the favourable direction shown (Northeast).

However, Horses should try to keep away from the unfavourable directions of the year – that is, South and North, as shown in Figure 1. Horses should try not to sit, work or sleep in these directions, so as to get rid of the negative influences lurking there.

Lucky Colours

According to Chinese tradition, each of the five elements has its own representative colours. Fire is represented by red, pink and purple, Earth by yellow and brown, and so on. As a Feng Shui Master I would suggest **orange, green** and **yellow** as Horse's lucky colours for the year 2002.

Use these colours in paints, wall coverings, rugs, drapes and curtains. This will be sure to bring good fortune within the year.

However, Horses should try not to use blue or grey in 2002, to avoid bad luck.

Lucky Numbers

The lucky numbers for Horses in 2002 are: **4** and **9**.

Fortune will be much improved by using these lucky numbers whenever possible. For example, if Horses have a choice, the phone number 244-9449 is better than 256-3377 – because the former contains more fours and nines, Horse's two lucky numbers for the year.

Lucky Charm

Feng Shui Masters believe that special objects can be used as a medium between human beings and nature. The fortune of the recipient is greatly improved as the positive wave of energy from nature is passed through the object or 'lucky charm' on to the recipient.

The lucky charm for the horse in 2002 is a pair of big peaches with three bats and two lotus leaves apiece. Peaches, in Chinese myth-ology, symbolize longevity while bats symbolize happiness. 'Two lotus leaves' sounds similar to 'year after year'. For best results it should be put in the southwest direction of the house.

Chapter Two

The
Sheep

Years of the Sheep

1907 (5/Feb/07—4/Feb/08)   1955 (4/Feb/55—4/Feb/56)
1919 (5/Feb/19—4/Feb/20)   1967 (4/Feb/67—4/Feb/68)
1931 (5/Feb/31—4/Feb/32)   1979 (4/Feb/79—4/Feb/80)
1943 (5/Feb/43—4/Feb/44)   1991 (4/Feb/91—3/Feb/92)

If you have any doubt about the classification of the 12 animal signs, or the divisions of months and years, please refer to pages xiii–xiv.

Distribution of the Stars within the Sign for 2002

Lucky Stars   Unlucky Star

The Sun   Black Cloud
Commander's Saddle
Union of the Year
Jade Hall

Lucky Stars

The Sun

The concept of Yin (female) and Yang (male) was essential in ancient Chinese culture. The Sun, representing energy and authority, is considered to be the most influential and important Yang symbol, similar to the god Apollo in Greek mythology.

When this Star appears for a Sign, evil things diminish just like snow melting under the warm sun.

Commander's Saddle

In ancient China, military commanders fought their battles on horseback. In battle a good saddle was essential for brave and effective fighting. As a result, the idea of a commander's saddle came to symbolize courage and military superiority.

Should this Star appear within the Sign, people can conquer life's obstacles if they are courageous enough. However, remember to be merciful towards defeated enemies.

Union of the Year

Unity is important for success. In the Chinese Horoscope, this Star harmonizes well with the year. Its appearance is a very good omen.

When this Star appears, people will be very popular and find it easy to win the friendship and support of those around them. Such good relations will bring handsome rewards in different projects and investments.

Jade Hall

In ancient China, thousands and thousands of scholars prepared for the Civil Service Examinations. However, only a few hundred of them ever passed, and would consequently be admitted to the ruling class. This newly-promoted elite would be deeply honoured with a big feast in a large decorated jade hall to celebrate their brilliant success.

When this Star appears, people will do well in their studies and in their work. They will have an important breakthrough if they work at it.

Unlucky Star
Black Cloud

Just as black clouds gather before a heavy rainstorm, unseen black clouds, the ancient Chinese believed, gathered just before the outbreak of disaster. Chinese fortune-tellers would look for these 'black clouds' in face- or palm-reading. When they appeared, it was said life would become less clear, and people would easily lose their way.

The appearance of this Star means that people must maintain a keen perspective on what is happening, or they will not be able to find their way out of disputes. During this period it is important to save money and energy for unexpected 'thunderstorms'.

General Overview of the Year

The appearance of several Lucky Stars within their Sign indicates that Sheep will have a pretty fortunate and productive year in 2002. They will have the wits and courage to encounter problems and challenges at work without too many difficulties. And there will be enough room at the top for them to move up if they are aggressive enough. Besides that, their popularity among their colleagues and friends will help them to see really splendid achievements at year end.

It's necessary for Sheep to try their best to keep up good business relationships throughout the year, or their chances of success will be badly hurt.

One thing that Sheep must bear in mind is that they must carry out their work by themselves all the way, because relying too much on others to take over their responsibilities would be a total failure. The appearance of the Lucky Star 'Jade Hall' indicates that Sheep will be very successful in different kinds of examinations, and will be able to win fame and fortune for themselves without too many difficulties.

Sheep will be quite fortunate in money affairs this year. They will be able to gain profits from different kinds of investments. If they wish to invest their money in new projects, this year will be a very good time for them to do so. Occasionally, Sheep will have some luck in lotteries and gambling, but they should try not to be too greedy about this.

The health of Sheep during this year will be in a fair condition. They don't have to worry about their health too much except for a few months in the middle of the year. If possible, Sheep should try to go on vacations to relax and refresh themselves several times during the year.

This will be a romantic year for Sheep. They will become quite popular, but they should remind themselves not to indulge in sex and entertainment too much, or both their health and career will be seriously damaged.

Career   * * * *
Money   * * *
Health   * *
Love   * * *

* * * * = Very Fortunate/ * * * = Pretty Good/ * * = Fair

Career * * * *

Sheep will have enough wit and energy to solve the problems and challenges at work without too much difficulty this year. Their outstanding performance will bring a promotion to them sooner or later. And there will be enough room at the top for Sheep to move up if they are aggressive enough. They would be even more successful if they wish to improve their relationships with their colleagues. Most important of all, Sheep must try to take care of their business by themselves as much as possible. The appearance of the Lucky Star 'Jade Hall' indicates that Sheep will be very successful in different kinds of examinations during the year.

However, Sheep will have some business problems during the first, third, seventh and the last two months of the year. It will be necessary for them to handle their work more seriously during these five months.

Money ***

Sheep will be quite fortunate in money affairs this year. Their investments will bring satisfactory profits to them, so this year would be a very good time for Sheep to invest their money in new projects. Occasionally, Sheep will have some luck in lotteries and gambling. Sheep will be more fortunate in money affairs during the second, fifth, eighth and ninth months. However, they should be more conservative in handling their money affairs during the third, sixth and the last two months of the year.

Health **

The health of Sheep will be in a satisfactory condition this year, but they should try not to exhaust themselves under a heavy working schedule. Taking breaks for vacations during the year will be the most effective way to relax and refresh themselves. Sheep must try to get enough rest and sleep during the fourth and seventh months. And they must watch out closely for their road safety during the tenth month. In addition, Sheep must be very careful about their food to prevent food poisoning or infections while travelling.

Love ***

Although this will be a romantic year for Sheep, they will have a lot of trouble at the same time too. Occasionally, Sheep will have quarrels and conflicts with their lover. It's necessary for them to reach a mutual understanding and respect in love affairs as soon as possible, or their relationships will break down sooner or later. The best thing for Sheep to do in this situation is to try to control their emotions and keep calm and silent in front of their irrational lovers if they don't want to mess up the whole thing. Sheep must pay more attention to solving problems in love affairs during the first, third, eighth, tenth and the last month of the year. However, they will have much better luck during the second, fifth and eleventh months.

Monthly In-depth Forecasts
The First Month (4 February – 5 March)

Pride goes before a fall

Although Sheep will have a much better year compared with 2001, they won't see a good beginning to the first month of the year. There will be numerous critics and challenges at work during this period, and Sheep will have a much better chance of survival if they stay humble throughout this time. Their personal pride and arrogance during this period will only lead them down the road of self-destruction in their careers. Sheep must try to give reasonable explanations for their decisions and to apologize sincerely for their mistakes and wrongdoings this month if they wish to get the necessary support from others at this critical moment. They would be in a much better situation by doing so. On the contrary, they would probably have a big fall sooner or later if they refused to do so.

Sheep won't have too much luck in love affairs this month. There will be serious arguments and quarrels between Sheep and their lovers during this period, and they should try to calm themselves. Things will get much better if Sheep try to reach a mutual understanding with their partner. Pride will only bring a broken relationship to Sheep at this stage.

This month, Sheep will save themselves from losing a lot of money in investments if they accept the opinions of others, especially of experts.

The Second Month (6 March – 4 April)

If a thing is worth doing, it's worth doing well

The luck of Sheep will be much improved this month, so that they should try their best at work during this period. In other words, Sheep should put extra time and effort into their careers, and stop fooling around, or they will miss several good business chances. They must keep in mind that 'if a thing is worth doing, it's worth doing well'. Sheep will probably be promoted at work by doing so. Their seriousness at work definitely won't be wasted.

This will be a very romantic month for Sheep. They have a very good chance of meeting someone very attractive at the beginning of the month. Although Sheep will become quite popular, they should not fool around with several lovers at the same time, or they will be very sorry about that in the months to come.

The fortune of Sheep in money affairs will be on an upward trend this month, and they will have pretty good luck in both investments and gambling. However, Sheep must keep alert, and protect themselves from being hurt by a robbery near the end of the month.

The Third Month (5 April – 5 May)

It takes two to make a quarrel

All of a sudden, bad luck will come as swiftly as a thunderstorm to Sheep this month. Sheep should try to keep their eyes wide open to watch their step, or they will have a sudden big fall in their careers. There will be numerous disputes and conflicts in and out of the office, and Sheep must try their best to settle them down with great patience. Sheep should not be reluctant to make a compromise with their opponents or competitors, because that will eventually save them a lot of trouble. It's really the time for Sheep to improve their personal and business relationships during this period of time, or their future success will be seriously damaged as a consequence.

This is definitely not a profitable month for Sheep. They will lose a lot of money if they try their luck in high-risk investments and gambling. It would be much better and safer if Sheep don't stay out too late at night during the last 10 days of the month.

Apart from this, Sheep must keep in mind that they should never try to start a quarrel or a fight with strangers at this critical moment.

Sheep should simply keep their mouths shut when they face their irritated lovers. It's necessary for them to walk away for a while before they lose patience with their lovers.

The Fourth Month (6 May – 5 June)

A trouble shared is a trouble halved

Fortunately, the bad luck of Sheep will disappear (albeit slowly) this month. But they still have as heavy a workload as last month, so they must work very hard to finish their daily tasks, or they will be left far behind. Actually, diligence alone can't solve all their problems; Sheep must try to get help from the people working around them. If they are able and willing to ask some other people to share their burdens, Sheep will thrive in their careers. That means Sheep should not refuse to ask for help for the sake of their pride, or their back will break under the heavy burden of their very tight working schedules. One thing Sheep should bear in mind is that they should never forget the people who lend them a helping hand at this critical moment.

The health of Sheep is not so good this month, and they must try to get enough rest and sleep after their hard work. Otherwise there might be a sudden collapse in health during the first 10 days of the month. Apart from this, Sheep must mind their safety in water. They must not try to risk their lives for the sake of fun and excitement when they go fishing, swimming or surfing.

The Fifth Month (6 June – 6 July)

Variety is the spice of life

This will be one of the most favourable months of the year for Sheep, so they'd better try to make good use of this period of time. Sheep will be full of confidence and energy in handling their daily work, and they will be quite productive so long as they don't waste time fooling around. Sheep should have the guts to make revolutionary changes in their careers, because they will have a very good chance of succeeding during this period. They should realize that their old habits and systems are somewhat outdated, and they will be certain losers if they refuse to make the necessary changes. Apart from this, Sheep should try to accept different kinds of proposals and different kinds of people at work, because these will broaden the foundations of their business for sure.

In love affairs, this is definitely a very romantic month for Sheep, and they will be busily engaged in different kinds of social gatherings. One thing they should keep in mind is that they should not turn a cold shoulder to new acquaintances with different opinions and backgrounds, or they will be very sorry about that very soon.

Although Sheep will be pretty lucky in money affairs this month, they should not put all their eggs in one basket. That means, they must try to diversify their investments in different areas.

The Sixth Month (7 July – 7 August)

Where there's a will, there's a way

Sheep will face serious challenges at work this month, but they must never give up under pressure or they will become the helpless victim of the cruel business world. As long as they can keep their determination strong, Sheep will be able to overcome most of their difficulties and challenges during this period of time. This is mainly due to the appearance of several Lucky Stars within their Sign. It's necessary for Sheep to hide their fears and weaknesses in front of their enemies at this critical moment. They must keep in mind that since they are going to have a very prosperous period in the second half of the year, they should not give up at this stage.

Although Sheep will have some luck in gambling, they should not be too greedy about this. Otherwise they will lose much more money than they'd ever anticipated during the last 10 days of the month. Apart from this, Sheep must try to pay their bills as soon as possible if they don't want to have endless trouble in the months to come.

In love affairs, Sheep should never give up even though they may be turned down by their loved ones several times. They should keep on trying to show their care and tenderness patiently and wisely. And they should remember that 'Where there's a will, there's a way.'

The Seventh Month (8 August – 7 September)

A little knowledge is a dangerous thing

This is one of the most difficult periods of the year for Sheep, in both their business and financial affairs. Probably, Sheep will find many changes in their working environment, and they had better try their best to adapt themselves as soon as possible. Otherwise, they will surely be eliminated sooner or later. Unless Sheep are willing to admit that they are ignorant of certain things, and try to do something about this, their ignorance will lead them to a total failure in their business.

Whether or not they can accept the advice of other, more experienced people will determine their chances of survival in their careers not only this month, but also for the months to come.

The health of Sheep will be quite weak this month, and they must try to see a doctor for proper medical treatments at once. It will be very dangerous for them to try to solve their health problems on their own.

This is definitely not a profitable month for Sheep. Probably, there will be more expenses than income during this period of time. Sheep should never try to make any investments instinctively, or they will have serious financial problems at the end of the year.

The Eighth Month (8 September – 7 October)

If the cap fits, wear it

The luck of Sheep will be much improved this month, and this is most obvious in their business lives. The difficulties and challenges of last month will mostly be gone, but they should watch out carefully for their business developments in order to make sure that their opponents don't try to attack them from behind during this period of time. However, their major concern of the month is to try to be more flexible at work, and try not to stick to the old dogma and systems. In other words, Sheep must face reality and try to adapt to it as soon as possible, even though they might have to give up something with which they are very familiar and comfortable. The more flexible Sheep are, the more successful they will be.

Sheep should not be too picky in friendships and love affairs this month, or they will be deeply disappointed. They will become somewhat isolated if they can't give up their prejudices.

This is one of the most fortunate months of the year for Sheep. They would have abundant income from different sources during this period of time. This month will be a very good time for Sheep to start a new joint venture in business, and this will bring handsome profits in the near future.

The Ninth Month (8 October – 6 November)

A carpenter is known by his chips

Sheep should be more serious in handling their daily work, because somebody will be watching them closely this month. They will be in big trouble if they fool around at work. However, if Sheep have tried their best in their work, they will surely win appreciation and admiration from their business circle. But they should keep in mind that only their actions, not empty words will bring them the appropriate fame. Since this will be a pretty fortunate month for Sheep, they wouldn't have any excuses if they were to fail in their careers.

Sheep will tend to talk too much in their private lives during this period of time. Their talkativeness will lead them to become a nuisance to their friends and lovers. Although this month is a favourable timing for vacations, Sheep should watch their diet carefully when travelling, to prevent infections.

Sheep will be quite fortunate in their investments this month. But they won't have the same luck in gambling and lotteries, so they must not risk their money on these matters or they will lose a lot of cash.

The Tenth Month (7 November – 6 December)

Actions speak louder than words

This will be one of the most favourable months of the year for Sheep. They will be very productive and successful at work during this period of time. However, Sheep should concentrate more on work than on empty talk, or they will miss several good chances. There will be lots of work, and Sheep will have to put extra time and effort in to finishing it, but they should not complain about this because the more they work, the more they get. Most important of all, Sheep have to show their ability and creativity if they wish to win the admiration and support of others in their business circle. In other words, their actions will be more persuasive than their words.

Sheep must walk and drive with extreme care in the early morning during the first 10 days of the month. Apart from this, they must try to stay away from heights to avoid a sudden big fall.

Sheep should not talk too much about their love affairs this month if they don't want to have unnecessary troubles. If it is possible, Sheep should spend more time with their family members during the weekends; this will bring them unforgettable memories in the years to come.

The Eleventh Month (7 December – 5 January)

Stretch your arm no further than your sleeve will reach

Because of the appearance of several Lucky Stars within the Sign this month, Sheep will be quite successful at work. However, Sheep should not be too aggressive about making a big leap, or they might experience a major fall next month. In other words, Sheep must do their job according to their own ability and never go beyond that, or they will collapse without any warning.

Somebody may use some attractive figures to invite Sheep for a joint venture, but they should simply turn down the offer if it's really beyond their capabilities. For the time being, Sheep should concentrate only on their own domestic business, and not waste time on foreign trades yet.

This month Sheep will have pretty good luck in love affairs. They will become quite popular. However, they must try not to make empty promises, or there will be endless trouble for them in the months to come.

Because their fortune in money affairs will be going up and down like a roller-coaster at the end of the month, Sheep must be more conservative in handling their financial affairs. They would be happier if they could find a way to be more easily contented.

The Twelfth Month (6 January – 3 February)

He who rides a tiger is afraid to dismount

Although Sheep have had much better luck overall this year, this month their luck is not so good. They will have to work very hard to survive in their careers, or they will be eliminated. Sheep must stand firm for themselves and never say die during this period of time. They will succeed if they stand firm and fight to the last. One thing Sheep should think about very carefully is that they must try their best to keep their promises, or they will become a sure loser in the cruel business world. This is definitely not a good time for Sheep to start any new projects or to change job, because they will face numerous obstacles and challenges. The best thing for them to do is to go step by step with their mouths shut in handling their daily work.

Sheep will meet with serious conflicts with their friends and lovers this month. They must try to control their temper and never let them get out of control, or they will be very sorry about that sooner or later.

This is definitely not a profitable month for Sheep, so they must stop risking their money in investments and gambling. Apart from this, Sheep should try to watch their expenses closely to make sure that these don't exceed their income at this critical moment.

Using Feng Shui to Improve Fortune: Directions, Colours, Numbers and Lucky Charm

The ancient Chinese used the traditional Horoscope to predict their fortune on a yearly basis – they used the art of Feng Shui to improve their luck.

It was their belief that the application of tactical Feng Shui would change their bad luck into good, and make their good luck improve even more.

This same method is still effective in today's modern world.

There are four main elements which I will use in tactical Feng Shui:

- Lucky Directions
- Lucky Colours
- Lucky Numbers
- Lucky Charm

Sheep will have a pretty fortunate and productive year in 2002. They will have the wit and courage to encounter challenges and difficulties at work without too many problems. And there will be enough room at the top for them to move up if they are aggressive enough. But they must try to take care of their business by themselves as much as they can, or the results will prove quite different. If they want to be more successful, Sheep must try to improve their business relationships throughout the year.

Fortunately, Sheep will be very successful at different kinds of examinations. In money affairs, Sheep will be quite fortunate both in investments and gambling, but they should not be too greedy.

Their health will be in a fair condition. If possible, Sheep should try to go on vacation to relax and refresh themselves several times during the year. Sheep will be quite popular socially, but they should remind themselves not to indulge too much in sex and alcohol. If they succumb to these temptations, both their health and career will be seriously damaged.

I would suggest applying the following Feng Shui tactics to ensure greater success throughout the year.

Lucky Directions

The most favourable directions of the year for Sheep are **South**, **West** and **Northwest**. Sheep should sleep or sit in these directions if they wish to improve their fortune.

To make this procedure very simple, divide the house or room into nine imaginary squares. Then, using a compass, check the exact direction of each square as shown in Figure 2. This will help to ensure that you do not make a mistake with the direction.

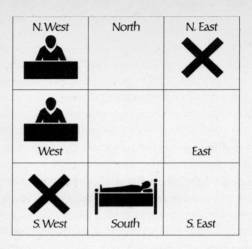

N. West	North	N. East
West		East
S. West	South	S. East

Figure 2

Sheep should sit in the West and Northwest at work or while studying; this will ensure that their achievements will be much greater than the Stars intended. To improve health and achieve a good night's sleep, Sheep should position the bed in the favourable direction shown (South).

However, Sheep should try to keep away from the unfavourable directions of the year – that is, Southwest and Northeast, as shown in Figure 2. Sheep should try not to sit, work or sleep in these directions, so as to get rid of the negative influences lurking there.

Lucky Colours

According to Chinese tradition, each of the five elements has its own representative colours. Fire is represented by red, pink and purple, Earth by yellow and brown, and so on. As a Feng Shui

Master I would suggest **blue, black** and **orange** as Sheep's lucky colours for the year 2002.

Use these colours in paints, wall coverings, rugs, drapes and curtains. This will be sure to bring good fortune within the year.

However, Sheep should not to use brown or green in 2002, to avoid bad luck.

Lucky Numbers

The lucky numbers for Sheep in 2002 are: **5** and **8**.

Fortune will be much improved by using these lucky numbers whenever possible. For example, if Sheep have a choice, the phone number 255-8558 is better than 247-9911 – because the former contains more fives and eights, Sheep's two lucky numbers for the year.

Lucky Charm

Feng Shui Masters believe that special objects can be used as a medium between human beings and nature. The fortune of the recipient is greatly improved as the positive wave of energy from nature is passed through the object or 'lucky charm' on to the recipient.

The lucky charm for the Sheep is a galloping horse with a running deer. Only the nobles and rich people could afford to ride on horses, so eventually horses came to be the symbol of fame and profits. 'Deer' in Chinese has the same pronunciation as 'official salary', so was considered to be the symbol of 'the ruling class' in the olden days. This lucky charm means 'to be rich and successful'. For best results, it should be put in the northwest direction of the house.

Chapter Three

The

Monkey

Years of the Monkey

1908 (5/Feb/08—3/Feb/09) 1956 (5/Feb/56—3/Feb/57)
1920 (5/Feb/20—3/Feb/21) 1968 (5/Feb/68—3/Feb/69)
1932 (5/Feb/32—3/Feb/33) 1980 (5/Feb/80—3/Feb/81)
1944 (5/Feb/44—3/Feb/45) 1992 (4/Feb/92—3/Feb/93)

If you have any doubt about the classification of the 12 animal
signs, or the divisions of months and years, please refer to pages
xiii–xiv.

Distribution of the Stars within the Sign for 2002

Lucky Star   Unlucky Stars

Travelling Horse   God of Loneliness
Funeral's Door

Lucky Star

Travelling Horse

In ancient China, travelling on horseback was the fastest and easiest way to get around. So, not surprisingly, the horse came to symbolize travel. Whether the journey would be smooth or not depended on the quality and condition of the horse.

When this Star appears it indicates that it is a good year to travel for both business and pleasure.

Unlucky Stars

God of Loneliness

In traditional Chinese society, living happily and harmoniously with other family members and friends was considered to be a great blessing. On the other hand, to live alone or to be ostracized by family or society was considered a horrible fate.

When this Star appears, people need to work on improving their relations with relatives, friends and colleagues, or they may be isolated.

Funeral's Door

In ancient China, funeral ceremonies were held at home. A pair of white lanterns would be hung outside to announce the death. The front door was kept closed to prevent unnecessary disturbances by those unconnected with the funeral. Since then, a tightly closed door with a pair of white lanterns has symbolized a grief-stricken family.

When this Star appears, people have to take care of their elderly family members by making sure that they receive proper medical treatment when required. In addition, they should pay more attention to their home safety.

General Overview of the Year

This will be a sluggish year for Monkeys, and it will be very difficult for them to see any important breakthroughs in their careers.

Unless Monkeys have very strong determination and wish to put in extra time and effort at work, their business will see no progress at all throughout the year. But Monkeys should never give up even though they are depressed and frustrated with their sluggish business. Instead, they should try to handle their business patiently and calmly, because the situation will become even worse if they lose heart (or their temper!). This year will not be a good time for Monkeys to make any drastic changes in business – that means, they should stay in their position and try to learn more to strengthen themselves quietly.

Monkeys must keep in mind that a capable and energetic partner will help them a lot in regaining their momentum at work during this year. And they will have a better chance of success if they start to develop their business in foreign places. As a matter of fact, Monkeys will travel quite a lot throughout the year. Their fortune in money affairs will be as sluggish as their business, however, so Monkeys should not expect too much in this area, or they will be deeply disappointed. It's necessary for Monkeys to cut down on their extravagant habits, and try to save as much money as they can. Gambling will lead them down the road of total self-destruction this year. If possible, Monkeys should try not to ask for any loans, or there will be endless troubles for them.

The appearance of the Unlucky Star 'Funeral's Door' indicates that Monkeys will be quite weak physically and mentally, so that they should try to take good care of themselves. Apart from this, Monkeys should not forget to watch out for the health and safety of their elderly family members, and try to get them immediate medical treatment if anything goes wrong with them.

This is definitely not a romantic year for Monkeys. Unless they try their best to show their care and tenderness towards their lovers, they may face a broken relationship sooner or later within the year.

Career	*
Money	**
Health	*
Love	*

** = Fair/* = Unsatisfactory

Career *

Monkeys have to struggle very hard to see any breakthroughs in their sluggish business. But they must not lose their patience in taking care of their business or the situation will become much worse. The best way for Monkeys in this situation is to try to stay at their own position and strengthen themselves through reading and studying quietly. If they are able to find a capable and energetic partner for themselves, Monkeys will be able to regain their momentum at work. The appearance of the Lucky Star 'Travelling Horse' indicates that Monkeys will travel quite a lot throughout the year, and they will have a better chance of success if they try to develop their business in foreign places this year. Monkeys will have better luck at work during the third, seventh, eighth and eleventh months. They should try to make good use of these four months if they wish to end the year having achieved something in business matters.

Money **

Monkeys should not expect too much in money affairs this year, or they will be deeply disappointed. They must try to keep to a tight budget to prevent their money from flowing away. They will become a sure loser if they try their luck in investments and gambling. One thing that Monkeys should keep in mind is that they should try not to get involved in loans and debt, or they will be in big trouble. However, Monkeys will be more fortunate during the third, seventh and eleventh months.

Health *

Unfortunately, the health of Monkeys will be quite weak both physically and mentally this year, so they should do their best to take care of themselves. If possible, Monkeys should try to take a break or vacation to rid themselves of continuous tension and anxiety. But they must try to have the necessary injections before their trips for the sake of their health. Apart from this, Monkeys have to take good care of their elderly family members too. Monkeys have to watch out for their own health during the second, sixth, seventh and tenth months. And they have to watch out for their safety during the first and fourth months.

Love *

Monkeys won't have too much luck in love affairs this year; it will be quite difficult for them to attract and impress others. Unless Monkeys show their care and tenderness towards their lovers sincerely, they will face a broken relationship. And they should keep in mind that they should never play with fire in their love affairs, or they will be very sorry about that in the coming years. However, Monkeys will have better luck in love affairs during the third, seventh, eighth and eleventh months.

If Monkeys are able to reach a mutual understanding with their lovers, their situation will be much improved.

Monthly In-depth Forecasts
The First Month (4 February – 5 March)

Haste is the road to hell

The first month of this year won't be a fortunate beginning for Monkeys. During this period of time, Monkeys will face numerous challenges and difficulties from different areas, so they must prepare themselves very well for the unexpected. It's very important for them to be more conservative in handling their business. In other words, Monkeys should go step by step to avoid a sudden big fall. They should think about their careers again and again before they come up with a decision. If Monkeys find out that things are getting out of control, they should not be reluctant to ask for help from those people who really care about them. This month is definitely not a good time for Monkeys to plan for their future development, because they simply don't have a keen perception and a clear mind during this period.

The fortune of Monkeys in money affairs will fluctuate from time to time this month, so they should not try their luck in high-risk investments.

Monkeys must drive with extreme care during the first half of the month, and they should keep in mind that 'Haste is the road to hell.' Better late than never.

The Second Month (6 March – 4 April)

Health is wealth

Because of the appearance of the Unlucky Star 'Funeral's Door' within their Sign, Monkeys must watch their health and safety carefully. No matter how hard they work, Monkeys must try to get as much rest and sleep as possible to avoid a sudden collapse. If there is anything wrong with their health, Monkeys must give up their work at once, and try to have the proper medical treatment without any delay. Monkeys must keep in mind that nothing is more important than their health. Without health, any amount of fame or money will be meaningless.

Other than that, Monkeys should try to keep to a healthy diet, too. This month Monkeys should try their best not to exhaust themselves. If possible, they should take a break or vacation to relax themselves. It would be a good time for Monkeys to improve their relationships and communications with their clients during this period. This will bring them a nice surprise in return.

This will not be a romantic month for Monkeys. They won't have too much luck in love affairs, but they should not be frustrated because this situation will change in the months to come.

The Third Month (5 April – 5 May)

Fortune favours the brave

The fortune of Monkeys will be much improved this month, so they should try to make good use of this period of time if they want to have better business achievements for this year. There will be a very good chance for them during this month, but it's all up to Monkeys whether to take it or not. If Monkeys dare to take this challenge, they will have a very good chance of success.

Otherwise, this opportunity will slip away through their fingers and never return. Apart from this, Monkeys should have the guts to make the necessary changes both in their business and financial systems this month, or they will meet with trouble in the very near future.

Monkeys will be quite fortunate in money affairs during this period of time. They will have an abundant income from different sources. However, they have to watch out for theft at month's end.

Monkeys will get a nice surprise if they have the guts to show their true feelings to their loved ones. Although they will be busily engaged in different social gatherings, they should not forget to spend some time with family members. It's necessary for Monkeys to take good care of the health and safety of elders at home, or they will be very sorry later on.

The Fourth Month (6 May – 5 June)

It takes all kinds to make a world

Monkeys will be bothered very much by numerous personal disputes and rumours this month. Unless they can handle these matters very well, their business will be seriously hurt. Better communications with people at work will be very important for Monkeys at this stage. Otherwise, it won't be possible for Monkeys to reach a mutual understanding and mutual trust with them. Most important of all, Monkeys should try to be open-minded, so they can accept different kinds of ideas and people.

Their moderate attitude will be the most effective remedy for their personal disputes at this stage.

Monkeys will be quite energetic this month, but they have to watch out for their safety when engaging in outdoor activities. They must pay extreme care regarding this, especially near the end of the month.

Monkeys tend to be quite jealous in their private lives, and this will seriously hurt their relationships with their lovers. They should be more open-minded in love affairs, or they will face a broken relationship sooner or later.

The Fifth Month (6 June – 6 July)

There's no smoke without fire

This will be one of the most unfavourable months of the year for Monkeys. They should keep their eyes wide open to watch for possible danger in their career. There will be no smoke without fire, so as soon as Monkeys smell the smoke, they must try their best to put out the fire at once. Apart from this, Monkeys should try to find out who their hidden enemies are around them, because probably they will be the people who set the fire in the first place. Most important of all, Monkeys must try to do their business according to all the relevant regulations and laws, and must not play any tricks during this period, or they will surely be punished.

This is definitely not a profitable month for Monkeys, so they must watch their expenses and investments closely or they will have money problems. They will lose a lot of money if they try their luck in any kind of gambling.

Monkeys will have a hot temper this month, and they have to calm themselves to avoid quarrels and even fights. It will be quite dangerous if Monkeys fail to do so.

The Sixth Month (7 July – 7 August)

Desperate diseases must have desperate remedies

Monkeys will face numerous problems and dangers at work, as was true last month, so they have to handle their business with extreme care.

Because of the appearances of several Unlucky Stars within their Sign, all the efforts of Monkeys may be in vain. No matter what happens, Monkeys must try to keep their confidence and never give up during this period of time. Even though Monkeys have tried several times without success before, they should try again this month. Just as the motto says, 'Desperate diseases must have desperate remedies.' Monkeys must try to apply unusual and drastic tactics to improve their troublesome business, or their careers will become hopeless.

During this period of time, Monkeys will be quite weak physically and mentally. It's very important for Monkeys to take good care of themselves. A well-balanced diet and adequate sleep will be the most effective remedies.

Unless Monkeys are able to do something about the leaks in their accounting systems at once, their financial situation will get worse and worse. Monkeys must try their best to keep away from money traps during the first 10 days of the month.

The Seventh Month (8 August – 7 September)

No pain, no gain

Although the luck of Monkeys will have improved a bit, they still have to work very hard for any breakthroughs in business. Probably, Monkeys will be busy running backwards and forwards, day and night during this period, but they should not complain about it. The more they work, the more they will get, and their efforts won't be wasted for sure. Monkeys will have no one to rely on but themselves at this stage, so they have to stand firm.

Fortunately, they will have much better luck at work over the next two months. This means that their stresses and strains at work will be much relieved in the near future. This month is a very good time for Monkeys to think about their plans for future development over the rest of the year.

Monkeys will have better luck in money affairs in the second half of the month, so they should not try their luck in investments or gambling in the first half, especially during the first ten days of the month.

Monkeys should try to take a break or vacation to refresh themselves this month. Probably, they will have a very good chance of meeting someone very attractive on their journeys. But they must watch their diet and try to keep away from raw meat and seafood.

The Eighth Month (8 September – 7 October)

Thought makes everything fit for use

This will be one of the most favourable months of the year for Monkeys. They will be very creative and productive at work during this period of time. If Monkeys are able to convert their creative ideas into practical use, their future development will have great potential. They must realize that they have to try to create something that is quite different from what everyone else is offering during this period. If they try to be a copycat, Monkeys will lose their future sooner or later. Museums, libraries, theatres, books, films and so on will inspire the imagination of Monkeys, so they should try to make good use of them.

Monkeys will be quite romantic this month, and they are longing for love. However, they must keep their eyes wide open to watch out for faithless lovers. Otherwise they will be easily cheated, and have endless trouble in the months to come.

This is definitely a profitable month for Monkeys. They will be able to find the right projects for investments, so they will have handsome shares from them in the near future. They will be pretty fortunate in lotteries and gambling in the middle of the month, but they should try not to be too greedy.

The Ninth Month (8 October – 6 November)

Seize the day

Monkeys will have a very busy work schedule during this month, so they must try their best to make use of every minute to finish their jobs or they will fall far behind their schedule. If they are just fooling around, their work will pile up and cause a lot of trouble in the near future. They should keep in mind that 'The sooner begun, the sooner done.' Any delay will be costly. Apart from this, Monkeys should try to respond quickly to requests, enquiries and complaints from their clients, government institutions or the public. The results will be much better if Monkeys can give an immediate response. Most important of all, if Monkeys fail to seize their opportunities on time, somebody else will take them away much sooner than they ever anticipated.

Generally speaking, seizing the day and seizing opportunities will be the major concerns of Monkeys during this period.

This is a bargaining month for Monkeys. They will be able to make a lot of money if they have strong persuasive powers. During the last 10 days of the month, Monkeys must try not to risk their money in gambling.

It's necessary for Monkeys to spend more time with their elderly family members this month, and watch their health and safety closely. In case there is anything wrong with family members, Monkeys must take them to the doctor or hospital.

The Tenth Month (7 November – 6 December)

It's the poor heart that never rejoices

Monkeys will become quite pessimistic and depressed this month, so it's very important for them to cheer themselves up. Otherwise, both their business and private life will be seriously hurt. Monkeys should try to think in a positive way even though they are in great difficulties. If not, Monkeys will discourage not only themselves, but the other people working with them. A team without spirit is as fragile as a group of soldiers without swords and shields. In other words, Monkeys should equip themselves and their fellow workers psychologically. Fortunately, Monkeys will hear some good news near the end of the month which will lighten their mood.

If possible, Monkeys should take a break or vacation to rid themselves of tension during this period. They must try to forget all about their worries and sorrows on their travels, or they will just waste their time and money. Monkeys should try to smile from the heart, because if they smile, the whole world will smile with them.

There will be numerous conflicts between Monkeys and their lovers this month. It's necessary for them to control their emotions if they don't want to have a broken relationship in the near future. If they will just say 'Sorry' to their lovers, the situation will become much better.

The Eleventh Month (7 December – 5 January)

Every cloud has a silver lining

Because of the appearance of several Lucky Stars within their Sign, this will be one of the most favourable months of the year for Monkeys. The bad luck of last month will disappear as swiftly as a storm, and a silver lining will begin to show up behind black clouds. Someone might lend a helping hand, and this will release much of the Monkey's burdens at work. More than that, there will be several offers made to them – it's up to Monkeys to make their own choice. However, Monkeys should try to be conservative about this because they are going to have problems in the coming month. The best thing for Monkeys to do during this period is to hope for the best and prepare for the worst.

This will be a very fortunate month in money affairs for Monkeys; they should try to make use of this period of time for different kinds of investments if they wish to see good profits in the near future. They should not try their luck at gambling at month's end.

There will be a rejuvenation of love affairs for Monkeys this month. That means Monkeys will have a second chance to mend a broken relationship. But they must take good care of it because it is very fragile at this stage.

The Twelfth Month (6 January – 3 February)

One bad apple spoils the whole barrel

All of a sudden, bad luck will come back again to Monkeys as swiftly as a thunderstorm this month. There will be numerous unexpected developments at work during this period of time. It's better for Monkeys to be cautious in handling their business. In other words, Monkeys should carry out their work step by step and try not to rush themselves to avoid a sudden big fall. Apart from this, Monkeys should never try to take on any work that's beyond their capabilities, or they will be in deep trouble in the months to come. Most important of all, Monkeys must try to get rid of incapable and faithless co-workers, bearing in mind the expression, 'one bad apple spoils the whole barrel'. Monkeys should take this action on this as soon as possible.

The fortune in money affairs of last month will totally fade away this month. If Monkeys are still dreaming of their luck in investments and gambling, they will become a sure loser. It's necessary for Monkeys to give up unprofitable investments as soon as possible, or the financial consequences will be terrible.

Fortunately, the health of Monkeys will be much improved this month. And they will have pretty good luck in love affairs, so they should not be shy about expressing their true feelings to their lovers.

Using Feng Shui to Improve Fortune: Directions, Colours, Numbers and Lucky Charm

The ancient Chinese used the traditional Horoscope to predict their fortune on a yearly basis – they used the art of Feng Shui to improve their luck.

It was their belief that the application of tactical Feng Shui would change their bad luck into good, and make their good luck improve even more.

This same method is still effective in today's modern world.

There are four main elements which I will use in tactical Feng Shui:

◆ Lucky Directions
◆ Lucky Colours
◆ Lucky Numbers
◆ Lucky Charm

Monkeys will have to struggle very hard for any important break-throughs in their sluggish business. It's necessary for them to handle this situation with extra effort and patience, or their jobs will be jeopardized. A capable and energetic partner will help them a lot in regaining their momentum in business. Apart from this, Monkeys should realize that they will have a better chance of success if they try to develop their business in foreign places.

Unfortunately, their fortune in money affairs will be sluggish, too. Monkeys must try to keep to a tight budget to avoid financial problems. Monkeys must try to keep away from gambling and loans this year, or they will be in big trouble. Monkeys will be quite weak physically and mentally; it's necessary for them to take good care of themselves. And they should not forget to watch the health and safety of elderly family members, too.

Monkeys won't have too much luck in love affairs this year. Unless they try their best to show their care and tenderness for their lovers sincerely, they may face a broken relationship.

I would suggest applying the following Feng Shui tactics to improve luck so Monkeys don't have to worry too much about their fate within the year.

Lucky Directions

The most favourable directions of the year for Monkeys are **Southeast, Southwest** and **North**. Monkeys should sleep or sit in these directions if they wish to improve their fortune.

To make this procedure very simple, divide the house or room into nine imaginary squares. Then, using a compass, check the exact direction of each square as shown in Figure 3. This will help to ensure that you do not make a mistake with the direction.

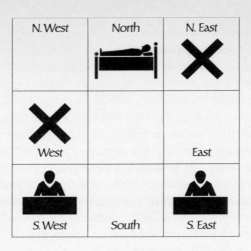

N. West	North	N. East
	🛏	✖
West		East
✖		
S. West	South	S. East

Figure 3

Monkeys should sit in the Southeast or Southwest at work or while studying; this will ensure that their achievements are much greater than the Stars intended. To improve health and achieve a good night's sleep, Monkeys should position the bed in the favourable direction shown (North).

However, Monkeys should try to keep away from the unfavourable directions of the year – that is, West and Northeast, as shown in Figure 3. Monkeys should try not to sit, work or sleep in these directions, so as to get rid of the negative influences lurking there.

Lucky Colours

According to Chinese tradition, each of the five elements has its own representative colours. Fire is represented by red, pink and purple, Earth by yellow and brown, and so on. As a Feng Shui Master I will suggest **pink**, **white**, **yellow** and **brown** as Monkey's lucky colours for the year 2002.

Use these colours in paints, wall coverings, rugs, drapes and curtains. This will be sure to bring good fortune within the year.

However, Monkeys should try not to use grey or black in 2002, to avoid bad luck.

Lucky Numbers

The lucky numbers for Monkeys are 1 and 7.

Fortune will be much improved by using these lucky numbers whenever possible. For example, if Monkeys have a choice, the phone number 271-1177 is better than 255-9866 – because the former contains more ones and sevens, Monkey's two lucky numbers for the year.

Lucky Charm

Feng Shui Masters believe that special objects can be used as a medium between human beings and nature. The fortune of the recipient is greatly improved as the positive wave of energy from nature is passed through the object or 'lucky charm' on to the recipient.

The lucky charm for the Monkey in 2002 is a pair of Kylin. Kylins, in Chinese mythology, are messengers that bring luck and fortune to human beings. Moreover, they scare the evils away. One of the Kylin is walking down from a stone with the Sun inscribed on it, while the other one is walking down from a stone with the Moon inscribed on it. For best results, this lucky charm should be put in the north direction of the house.

Chapter Four

The

Rooster

Years of the Rooster

1909 (4/Feb/09—3/Feb/10)   1957 (4/Feb/57—3/Feb/58)
1921 (4/Feb/21—3/Feb/22)   1969 (4/Feb/69—3/Feb/70)
1933 (4/Feb/33—3/Feb/34)   1981 (4/Feb/81—3/Feb/82)
1945 (4/Feb/45—3/Feb/46)   1993 (4/Feb/93—3/Feb/94)

If you have any doubt about the classification of the 12 animal signs, or the divisions of months and years, please refer to pages xiii–xiv.

Distribution of the Stars within the Sign for 2002

Lucky Stars	Unlucky Stars
Pink Phoenix	Hooked and Strained
The Moon	Sudden Death
	Six Harms
	Tightened Loop

Lucky Stars
Pink Phoenix

In traditional Chinese culture phoenixes were legendary, mystical birds, famous for spending time in romantic, affectionate pairs. Over time the phoenix came to symbolize love and marriage, and for centuries it has been included in Chinese wedding ceremonies.

The appearance of this Star is a very good omen. It indicates a romantic year with good marriage possibilities.

The Moon

The concept of Yin (female) and Yang (male) is very strong in Chinese culture. Just as the Sun symbolizes Yang, the Moon for centuries has symbolized Yin.

The appearance of this Star is a good omen because it will brighten up life just as the Moon brightens up the world at night.

Unlucky Stars
Hooked and Strained

Being hooked by sharp objects or strained by ropes are definitely very terrible experiences. Unfortunately, this Star is somewhat related with these two dire events.

The appearance of this Star is a bad omen. People have to be very careful every step of the way in order to avoid risking their lives within the year.

Sudden Death

Due to the inadequate knowledge of medicine in ancient China, a lot of sudden deaths were believed to be caused by the unpredictable will of the gods. This kind of ignorance kept many from trying to get medical care when they needed it.

This Star is one of the worst Unlucky Stars in the Chinese Horoscope. When this Star appears within a Sign, people have to keep all medical appointments and try to take preventative measures before it is too late.

To the ancient Chinese peasants, floods, drought, frost, wars, plagues of locusts and other insects and so on were the major harms faced by their crops. The occurrence of any one of these harms would seriously damage their income. The appearance of the Star 'Six Harms' is a very bad omen to the economy of the people concerned.

When this Star appears within a Sign, people have to watch out for the economic growth of their business, and for sudden changes such as a dramatic drop in sales and production or cancellation of contracts, etc.

Tightened Loop

Loops were commonly used by the ancient Chinese to catch animals. Consequently, a loop is usually considered to be the symbol of a trap. A person, as well as an animal, might get caught or even strangled by a tightened loop. So it is better to stay away from any kind of traps.

The appearance of this Star is a warning signal. People have to keep their eyes wide open to watch out for the traps in front of them. Otherwise, it will prove very difficult to get out of the traps and dilemmas.

General Overview of the Year

Roosters will have to keep their eyes wide open to watch out for business traps this year, or they will not only lose a lot of money, but their reputations will suffer as well. The appearance of the two Unlucky Stars 'Tightened Loop' and 'Hooked and Strained' within their Sign indicates that Roosters will be easily caught by traps and become helpless victims if they don't know how to protect themselves. If possible, Roosters should try to ask for advice from experienced consultants to avoid being cheated. Apart from this, Roosters should try to be more flexible in handling their business if they wish to be able to survive this tough year. It would be a big help to their business development if Roosters were able to set up clear goals to work towards, and a clever strategy to carry them through. Most important of all, Roosters should never try to go too far beyond their work and financial abilities in business, or they will face total failure at the year end.

This is definitely not a profitable year for Roosters. They must watch their budgets and try to be more conservative in investments to avoid a sudden financial collapse. Apart from this, Roosters have to keep on checking the economic growth of their business developments to catch any sudden drop in sales, sudden cash shortage and so on. Money traps will be a continuous threat to Roosters throughout the year.

Generally speaking, Roosters' health will be in a satisfactory condition. But due to the appearance of the Unlucky Star 'Sudden Death' within the Sign, Roosters should try to pay more attention to their personal safety to avoid a serious accident.

Roosters will have a very romantic year in 2002. If they are looking for true love or a happy marriage, their dreams will come true. However, Roosters should try not to let their private affairs mess up their business affairs, or they will spoil both.

Career	*
Money	**
Health	**
Love	****

**** = Very Fortunate/** = Fair/* = Unsatisfactory

Career *

There will be some business traps around them, so that Roosters should try to keep their eyes wide open to avoid them, or they will not only lose their money, but their reputations too. If possible, Roosters should try to listen to the suggestions of some other people or to take professional advice from experienced experts to avoid being cheated. Roosters will have a better chance of survival if they are able to set up clear goals and plan well for their business developments at the beginning of the year. Most important of all, Roosters should not be too ambitious at work, and never try to go too far beyond their working and financial abilities. Roosters will have better luck in business during the third, fifth, seventh, tenth and the last month of the year; they should try to make good use of these times.

Money **

Roosters won't have too much luck in money affairs. Although they will have a steady income, they might face a sudden financial collapse some time during the year. Two things that Roosters must consider very carefully: first, keep away from money traps, and second, don't go too far beyond their financial abilities. Otherwise, Roosters will be in a very terrible financial situation. Roosters must keep alert to money affairs during the second, fifth, sixth, eighth, ninth and eleventh months.

Health **

The appearance of the Unlucky Star 'Sudden Death' indicates that Roosters must try to pay more attention to their health and safety during this year. It's necessary for Roosters to watch their diet and personal hygiene closely. If anything goes wrong with them, Roosters must try to go to the doctor for proper medical treatment as soon as possible. Most important of all, Roosters must pay more attention to their safety when engaged in outdoor activities to avoid serious injury. Roosters must watch their safety during the first and ninth months. Apart from this, they must try to get enough rest and sleep to avoid exhaustion during the third, fifth and last month of the year. They should also take good care of younger family members at home during the tenth month.

Love ★★★★

Roosters will become very popular this year. If they are looking for true love or a happy marriage, their dreams will come true. However, Roosters should pay more attention to their love affairs during the first, third, sixth, seventh and ninth months. Although somebody may try to step in between Roosters and their lovers, fortunately they will be able to be the winner and keep their sweet relationship. But they should not show off too much about their romance, or there will be endless trouble not only this year, but also for the coming years too.

Monthly In-depth Forecasts
The First Month (4 February – 5 March)

Living without an aim is like sailing without a compass

Unfortunately, Roosters won't see a good start to the year, so that they should try to put more time and effort in at work if they don't want to be left too far behind the others. Although diligence is key to their career survival, Roosters should not forget to set targets for future development. Roosters must think about the expression, 'Living without an aim is like sailing without a compass.' Failure to set up targets for the future will not only confuse Roosters, but will also confuse the people working with them, and that would be very dangerous. If necessary, Roosters must not be reluctant to ask the opinions and advice of experts for their business plans for the whole year.

This won't be a romantic month for Roosters, and probably they will be frustrated in their love affairs. However, they should take it easy or there will be heart-break for them sooner or later.

Although Roosters will be quite healthy this month, they must mind their safety carefully in water, especially on the open seas. They should also watch for changes in the weather and never risk their lives out of a sense of curiosity or in search of excitement.

The Second Month (6 March – 4 April)

Human pride is human weakness

This is one of the most unfavourable months of the year for Roosters. Numerous difficulties and personal disputes will keep on bothering them from time to time during this period, so that Roosters must try their best to settle them with patience and never let them get out of control. This will probably be too much for Roosters to deal with single-handed, so it's necessary for them to give up their pride and ask for help from others, such as colleagues, associates or friends. Their chance of survival at work will be doubled by doing so. If they do not, Roosters will be easily defeated and become helpless victims under the shadow of their enemies. Apart from this, Roosters must avoid being arrogant at work, or they will surely be ostracized.

Somebody may try to use some tricks to cheat Roosters in money affairs during the first 10 days of the month. Therefore, they should keep their eyes wide open and keep away from money traps.

Roosters will be quite weak physically during this period of time. It's very important for them to try to get enough rest and sleep to avoid a collapse in health. If possible, Roosters should try to take a break or vacation to refresh themselves.

The Third Month (5 April – 5 May)

Great minds think alike

If Roosters can improve their business and personal relationships, this will be a productive and successful month for them. Roosters will be loaded with creativity and energy this month, but it will all be wasted if they fail to make use of it at work. Apart from this, Roosters should look beyond the workplace for potential partners in their future business development. They will see splendid achievements in the months to come if they can find a sincere and capable partner who shares their goals. One thing that Roosters must bear in mind is that they should be able to tolerate opposing ideas, otherwise there will be endless trouble for them sooner or later.

Roosters should keep their mouth shut and a smile on their face this month. They should be open-minded in love affairs, and try not to be so jealous. Unless they wish to terminate their relationships, Roosters should forgive and forget the wrong-doings of their lovers. Their tolerance will pay off very soon.

The health and fortune of Roosters will be much improved this month, and they should take it easy in their private lives. However, Roosters should not spend too much money on alcohol or sex, or both their health and fortune will be seriously hurt.

The Fourth Month (6 May – 5 June)

Cut your coat according to your cloth

Roosters must try to curb their ambition this month, or they will have big troubles in the months to come. Although Roosters will be full of confidence about their projects, they should try to think about them carefully one by one to see whether they are beyond their abilities or not. If their projects are really beyond their working or financial capabilities, Roosters must put a halt to them at once. However, Roosters will be able to enjoy a comfortable working atmosphere if they are content with their present job. Most important of all, Roosters must pay more attention to the quality control of their products, or there will be cancellations of contracts, or claims made against their products for different reasons in the months to come.

This month will be a good time for Roosters to buy property and valuables. And they will have some luck in lotteries and with gambling too. But there will be some troubles in their investments, so they should keep an eye on them closely.

Roosters will have a very good chance to meet someone very attractive this month, but they should try to consider whether they really match each other or not. Otherwise, they should forget about the whole thing as soon as possible, or they will be in deep sorrow sooner or later.

The Fifth Month (6 June – 6 July)

A live dog is better than a dead lion

Roosters will be quite weak both physically and mentally this month, so that it will be very important for them to try to get as much rest and sleep as possible. Otherwise, there may be a collapse in health under the pressure of heavy work. If there is anything wrong with them, Roosters must try to get the proper medical treatment at once without any delay, because failure to do so will have very serious consequences. One thing that Roosters must bear in mind is that they should not exhaust themselves at any cost during this period of time, or they will be very sorry about that in the near future.

Roosters will have some problems at work this month. Fortunately, they will be able to overcome most of them. Roosters should watch those small but active opponents, because they will cause more trouble than the big but not-so-active ones.

Regarding investments, Roosters must consider all angles carefully before they make up their minds; hasty decisions will only lead them to self-destruction. Most important of all, they must forget about gambling at the end of the month.

The Sixth Month (7 July – 7 August)

Bad money drives out good

Bad luck will come as swiftly as thunderstorms this month, so that Roosters must know how to protect themselves at this critical moment or they will be eliminated from their career.

No matter how hard they try, Roosters will have simply no luck at work if they don't know the tricks of their business. Roosters should consult with experienced colleagues if they want to survive the storm. Apart from this, Roosters should watch for hidden enemies around them. Unless Roosters are able to prevent being attacked from behind, they will become helpless victims. It's so cruel and so true that bad money often drives out good. Roosters must try to prevent such a terrible situation from happening to them.

This is definitely not a profitable month for Roosters; it would be much better for them to stop their investments and gambling for the time being. In addition, they must watch out for money traps, or they will lose a lot of cash.

Probably, there will be a stranger stepping in between Roosters and their lovers this month. Roosters will suffer a lot if they don't pay enough attention to this new situation. Something unexpected may happen in love affairs without any warning.

The Seventh Month (8 August – 7 September)

When things are at their worst, they begin to mend

The thunderstorm of last month will begin to fade gradually this month, and Roosters will have much better luck in both their business and private life. Opportunities will keep on knocking at the door during this period, so Roosters should keep their eyes wide open and not let any chances slip through their fingers. It's time for Roosters to try to pick up their momentum again at this stage; if they can do so, they will be quite successful without too much difficulty. But Roosters must bear in mind that they must not play tricks, or all their efforts will be in vain. If they break any regulation or law, Roosters will surely be punished for that sooner or later.

Relations between Roosters and their lovers will be improving throughout the month. Their romance will turn over a new leaf during this period. Roosters should try to avoid political topics with new acquaintances at social gatherings during the first 10 days of the month.

Fortune in money affairs will be much improved this month, and Roosters will be able to get more income from different sources. Their luck in lotteries and gambling will be quite good in the middle of the month.

The Eighth Month (8 September – 7 October)

You can't tell a book by its cover

The luck of Roosters will be on a downward trend this month, so they should keep their eyes wide open to prevent things from getting out of control. The sooner, the better. Apart from this, Roosters should have a keen perception about their business and the people within their business circle. They will lose a lot of money if they fail to do so. Roosters must bear in mind that 'Appearances are deceptive.' They must try their best not to listen to flattery during this period, or they will be easily cheated.

The fortune of Roosters will be going up and down like a roller-coaster, so that it will be much safer if they are more conservative in handling their financial affairs. They must try to save as much as they can for the rainy days ahead in the months to come.

Roosters will have several choices in love affairs during this period, but they should try not to make decisions in a rush. Most important of all, they should not judge by appearances only, or they will be very sorry about that in the near future.

The Ninth Month (8 October – 6 November)

Bad news travels fast

This is one of the most unfavourable months of the year for Roosters. There will be numerous difficulties at work, and they will be exhausted by their heavy workload. Therefore, it's necessary for them to know how to pace themselves, particularly during the first half of the month. Roosters will be big losers if they fail to do so.

There might be some bad news from foreign places or overseas. Roosters should not worry about this too much because it's somewhat beyond their control anyway. One thing Roosters must keep in mind is that they should try to keep a low profile and try not to create any news, because no news is good news for them this month.

Fortune in money affairs will be very terrible for Roosters. Unless they can watch their expenses very closely, they will have financial problems not only this month, but also in the months to come.

There will be numerous rumours and gossip about Roosters this month. Roosters will suffer from endless trouble if they can't handle this properly. The best thing for them to do is try not to show off too much, and say nothing of their romance at this critical moment.

The Tenth Month (7 November – 6 December)

Business before pleasure

The luck of Roosters has been quite unstable during this year. Now, all of a sudden, the difficulties and sorrows in both their business and private life will go with the wind. Roosters will be very productive at work this month, and they will get the necessary help and support from others whenever needed. But they should not forget that they are the real architects of their own fate during this period. In other words, Roosters must work very hard for their success in business, or they will just spoil their opportunities. 'Business before pleasure' is the key to success right now. This month will be a very good time for Roosters to broaden their mind through reading and studying, because it will be much easier for them to absorb different kinds of knowledge.

Roosters must try not to indulge themselves too much in sex and alcohol this month, or their career will be seriously hurt. Roosters must keep in mind that they should not let their private life get mixed up with their business life.

The health of Roosters will be much improved this month. However, they have to take care of youngsters at home very conscientiously. If anything goes wrong with them, Roosters must try to take them to the doctor to get proper medical treatment as soon as possible.

The Eleventh Month (7 December – 5 January)

What can't be cured must be endured

Roosters may face a broken relationship with their lovers this month. However, they must not bury themselves in grief, or both their career and health will be seriously hurt. In this situation, Roosters should not forget the motto, 'Let bygones be bygones.' Probably, their romantic life will turn over a new leaf at year's end, so they should try their best to cheer themselves up.

At work, Roosters might be badly defeated by their opponents or rejected by their superiors this month. Yet they must not lose their confidence or determination. As long as they keep on trying, Roosters will have a good chance of survival in business at year's end.

Roosters must stop thinking of their previous losses in investments or gambling. Instead, they should think about how to start all over again with caution. It's also time for Roosters to curb their extravagant habits.

The health of Roosters won't be too good this month. They will be easily bothered by infections during this period. It's necessary for them to keep away from crowded places with unhealthy air, or they will face endless health problems in the months to come.

The Twelfth Month (6 January – 3 February)

The darkest hour is just before dawn

Although this hasn't been a very fortunate year for Roosters, fortunately they will have a pretty good end to the year at work. Their suffering at the hands of last month's heavy workload will finally come to an end. It's time for Roosters to think about future development for the coming years. But they should not forget to choose a dependable partner to work with, or their chances of success will be much diminished.

Roosters must not rush themselves at work in order to avoid a sudden big fall. Just like a sick person must recover slowly, step by step, Roosters will emerge only gradually after the dark hours in business over the past few months.

Roosters will have a very good chance to meet someone lovely this month, and they will very much enjoy this new romance. However, Roosters should not push too much or they will scare away their new acquaintances. This month will be a very good time for Roosters to improve their relationships with colleagues and neighbours.

Although the health of Roosters is improving, they must watch their diet carefully to avoid food poisoning.

Fortunately, Roosters will have some luck in investments, but not in gambling during this period of time.

Using Feng Shui to Improve Fortune: Directions, Colours, Numbers and Lucky Charm

The ancient Chinese used the traditional Horoscope to predict their fortune on a yearly basis – they used the art of Feng Shui to improve their luck.

It was their belief that the application of tactical Feng Shui would change their bad luck into good, and make their good luck improve even more.

This same method is still effective in today's modern world.

There are four main elements which I will use in tactical Feng Shui:

- ◆ Lucky Directions
- ◆ Lucky Colours
- ◆ Lucky Numbers
- ◆ Lucky Charm

Roosters will face several business traps around them, so they must try to keep their eyes wide open or they will become helpless victims this year. Because Roosters will be easily confused, it's necessary for them to ask for professional advice from experienced experts to avoid being cheated. Most important of all, Roosters must try not to be too ambitious or to go beyond their own capabilities, or they might suffer a sudden big fall in business.

Because this won't be a profitable year for Roosters, they must be more conservative in their budgeting. And, of course, they must try to keep away from money traps or they will lose a lot of money.

Due to the appearance of the Unlucky Star 'Sudden Death', Roosters must pay more attention to their health and safety. They must try to get enough rest and sleep to avoid a sudden collapse in health.

Fortunately, Roosters will have a sweet and romantic year. If they are looking for true love or a happy marriage, their dreams will come true.

I would suggest applying the following Feng Shui tactics to improve luck so Roosters don't have to worry too much about their fate within the year.

Lucky Directions

The most favourable directions of the year for Roosters are **Southeast**, **West** and **Northeast**. Roosters should sleep or sit in these directions if they wish to improve their fortune.

To make this procedure very simple, divide the house or room into nine imaginary squares. Then, using a compass, check the exact direction of each square as shown in Figure 4. This will help to ensure that you do not make a mistake with the direction.

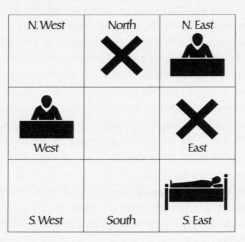

Figure 4

Roosters should sit in the West and Northeast at work or while studying; this will ensure that their achievements are much greater than the Stars intended. To improve health and achieve a good night's sleep, Roosters should position the bed in the favourable direction shown (Southeast).

However, Roosters should try to keep away from the unfavourable directions of the year – that is, East and North, as shown in Figure 4. Roosters should try not to sit, work or sleep in these directions, so as to get rid of the negative influences lurking there.

Lucky Colours

According to Chinese tradition, each of the five elements has its own representative colours. Fire is represented by red, pink and purple, Earth by yellow and brown, and so on. As a Feng Shui Master I would suggest **green, white** and **brown** as Rooster's lucky colours for the year 2002.

Use these colours in paints, wall coverings, rugs, drapes and curtains. This will be sure to bring good fortune within the year.

However, Roosters should not use red and orange in 2002, to avoid bad luck.

Lucky Numbers

The lucky numbers for Roosters in 2002 are: 2 and 4.

Fortune will be much improved by using these lucky numbers whenever possible. For example, if Roosters have a choice, the phone number 244-4224 is better than 235-6699 – because the former contains more twos and fours, Rooster's two lucky numbers for the year.

Lucky Charm

Feng Shui Masters believe that special objects can be used as a medium between human beings and nature. The fortune of the recipient is greatly improved as the positive wave of energy from nature is passed through the object or 'lucky charm' on to the recipient.

The lucky charm for the Rooster in 2002 is a statue with three goats walking out from a huge stone. 'Goat' has the same pronunciation as 'male' and 'sun', so this statue symbolizes power and bright future. For best results, it should be put in the southeast direction of the house.

Chapter Five

The
Dog

Years of the Dog

1910 (4/Feb/10—4/Feb/11)   1958 (4/Feb/58—3/Feb/59)
1922 (4/Feb/22—4/Feb/23)   1970 (4/Feb/70—3/Feb/71)
1934 (4/Feb/34—4/Feb/35)   1982 (4/Feb/82—3/Feb/83)
1946 (4/Feb/46—3/Feb/47)   1994 (4/Feb/94—3/Feb/95)

If you have any doubt about the classification of the 12 animal
signs, or the divisions of months and years, please refer to pages
xiii–xiv.

Distribution of the Stars
within the Sign for 2002

Lucky Stars	Unlucky Stars
The Three Pillars	Yellow Funeral Flag
Earthly Salvation	Decorative Top
	Five Ghosts
	Flying Spell
	Legal Spell
	Loose Hair

Lucky Stars
The Three Pillars

In ancient China, the *Ding* was a large and heavy cooking pot supported by three strong legs. As the Ding has been used to symbolize the government, the three legs have symbolized the three prime ministers of the government, who worked as the solid support of the whole country. These ministers possessed absolute power to keep everything under control.

The appearance of this Star is a very good omen. It indicates enough confidence and strength to overcome opponents and challengers, and triumph if a person commits him- or her-self to a goal.

Earthly Salvation

There are three 'Salvation' Stars in the Chinese Horoscope: 'Heavenly Salvation', 'Earthly Salvation' and 'God of Salvation'. They are all considered to have the power to help people out of trouble and disasters. Among the three, 'Earthly Salvation' is the least important. Still, its appearance is a good omen for those in trouble.

When this Star appears, people's suffering will be alleviated. Nonetheless, people should still try to keep themselves out of difficulty, since the Star's influence is not so strong.

Unlucky Stars
Yellow Funeral Flag

In ancient times, the Chinese believed that the spirits of the newly dead floated aimlessly in the sky. To guide the spirits back home, their families would fly a yellow flag from the rooftop to signal where they lived. Not surprisingly, yellow flags soon become a symbol for death and funerals.

When this Star appears, people need to be extra careful about the health and safety of younger family members. Keep in mind that 'prevention is better than cure'.

Decorative Top

In ancient China, only the nobles and important people were allowed to cover the tops of their carriages with rich decoration, which varied according to rank. Such decorated carriages naturally became associated with high social status, luxury and, interestingly enough, with a certain degree of isolation typical of those who inhabit their own exclusive world away from the masses.

Thus, the implications of this Star are ambiguous. On the one hand, when this Star appears people will enjoy a successful year; on the other, they will have a tendency to become isolated if they do not remain connected in their personal relationships.

Five Ghosts

The Chinese believe that ghosts are best avoided, since they threaten people's health and safety. To living people, meeting five ghosts at once would definitely be a horrible experience. Surely, then, this Star is not a good omen.

The appearance of this Star is a warning to play it safe. Avoid provoking anyone in a position of authority, or it could lead to an endless nightmare.

Flying Spell

In ancient times, Chinese magic spells were created through special symbols and characters written by Taoist priests in red ink or even blood. Based on this, the concept of five 'Evil Spell' Stars in the Chinese Horoscope developed. This is one of them.

As its name suggests, the Flying Spell was the kind that flew through the sky, invisible to the human eye. When someone experienced bad luck, it was blamed on an unfortunate encounter with such a flying spell.

When this Star appears, people should try to keep a low profile and be alert to prepare for unexpected troubles or even accidents.

Legal Spell

This is one of the five 'Magic Spell' Stars in the Chinese Horoscope. The ancient Chinese believed that the family would get entangled in lawsuits as a result of an encounter with this spell.

When this Star appears, people need to watch their conduct and follow the rules. They should be very careful in managing their affairs, to avoid legal problems or lawsuits.

Loose Hair

After the age of 20, Chinese noblemen and gentry would grow their hair long, wearing it tied up in a knot at the top of their head. However, during periods of mourning for the death of a family member they would let their hair fall down like a waterfall to show that they were too filled with sorrow to worry about their personal appearance.

This Star is a bad omen. If it appears within a Sign, remember to take care of younger family members and keep an eye on safety at home.

General Overview of the Year

This will be a very busy year for Dogs, so they have to put in more time and effort at work. They will be able to enjoy splendid achievements at the end of the year after a long, hard struggle. But they should understand that there will be no free lunch, and their success will stay out of reach if they're not prepared to sweat for it. Dogs will have enough energy and wit to solve almost all of their problems at work, but they should not forget to settle disputes and conflicts between their colleagues and themselves. Otherwise they will be isolated and become the target of scorn.

Because of the appearance of the Unlucky Star 'Legal Spell', Dogs will easily get involved in legal problems this year. Dogs must not take risks with the law, or they will surely be punished or even end up in gaol. It's necessary for them to keep away from their wicked false friends, or their future will be spoiled.

Fortunately, Dogs will have pretty good luck in money affairs. Their investments will bring satisfactory profits to them, and their regular income will be quite steady this year, so that they don't have too much to worry about in financial matters. But they should try not to risk their money in gambling or lotteries, or their hard-earned cash will be gone with the wind.

There won't be too many health problems for Dogs, but they should try to take breaks or holidays to release themselves from the continuous tension and avoid a nervous breakdown. Most important of all, the appearance of the two Unlucky Stars 'Yellow Funeral Flag' and 'Loose Hair' indicates that Dogs must take good care of younger family members, and try to get them proper medical treatment as soon as anything goes wrong with them.

Although Dogs will be quite popular, unfortunately they will probably be deeply disappointed if they are looking for true love this year. Unless Dogs wish to give up their pride and arrogance, their friends and lovers will walk away from them.

Career	***
Money	***
Health	**
Love	**

*** = Pretty Good/** = Fair

Career ***

Dogs will be very busy at work because there will be a heavy workload for them to handle this year. Fortunately, they could enjoy splendid achievements at the end of the year after a long, hard struggle.

Dogs will have enough energy and wit to solve most of their business problems, but their chances of success will be seriously hurt if they fail to settle personal disputes and conflicts between their colleagues and themselves. Dogs have to remind themselves not to break any laws under any situation, or they will surely get tangled up in legal problems, or even end up in gaol. Dogs should pay more attention to their business development during the second, third, fourth, sixth, eighth and eleventh months.

Money * * *

Dogs will have pretty good luck in money affairs. They will have a satisfactory regular income this year, but their luck in lotteries and gambling will be terrible. They will become a sure loser if they try to risk their money this year. If possible, Dogs must try to pay all their bills promptly to avoid endless trouble in the future. Dogs have to keep their eyes wide open to watch out for their money during the second, third, sixth, eighth and eleventh months. They should be more conservative in handling their investments and budgets during these five months.

Health * *

Physically, Dogs won't have too many problems this year, but they will be quite weak mentally because of the continuous tension brought on by a very tight work schedule. Therefore, it's necessary for Dogs to take vacations to refresh themselves and avoid a nervous breakdown.

Enough rest and sleep will be the most effective remedy for Dogs during the year. Apart from this, Dogs must watch out for the health and safety of younger family members at home very closely. Any negligence will be dangerous.

Dogs have to take care of themselves during the fourth and eighth months. And they must pay special attention to taking care of their children during the tenth month. It's necessary to keep drugs and dangerous sharp objects, such as knives and scissors, out of the reach of the children at home.

Love **

Dogs will be quite attractive this year, but it won't be easy for them to find true love. They should try not to fool around with several partners at the same time, or they will have endless trouble as a consequence. Most important of all, Dogs should never let their personal affairs get mixed up with their business, or both will surely be spoiled. Having said this, Dogs will have much better luck in love affairs during the first, fifth, ninth and the last month of the year. They should try to make good use of these four months.

Monthly In-depth Forecasts
The First Month (4 February – 5 March)

Where bees are, there is honey

Because of the appearance of several Lucky Stars within the Sign, Dogs will see a pretty fortunate start to the year. They will be very productive and successful if they work hard enough without too many interruptions. Although they will have a very busy schedule at work, Dogs should not complain too much about this, because the more they work, the more they get. Their efforts during this period surely won't be wasted. Dogs must keep in mind that they should always put work before pleasure, or they will waste several opportunities this month.

Dogs will be even more successful if they are able to stimulate the enthusiasm of co-workers.

This will be a very romantic month for Dogs, but they should not indulge themselves too much in love affairs. They should never let their private lives get mixed up with their business.

Dogs will have some luck in lotteries and gambling during the first 10 days of the month. But, unfortunately, their luck in investments won't be too good at this stage. Apart from this, Dogs must watch out for their valuables at the end of the month, or they will suffer a burglary.

The Second Month (6 March – 4 April)

Hope deferred makes the heart sick

Dogs won't have the same luck as last month, and they might end up with nothing after a very hard struggle at work during this period of time. Dogs shouldn't give up at this stage, or they won't have a second chance to start over again. In other words, persistence will be the key to their survival in business. Most important of all, Dogs must try to keep their promises. They will lose the necessary support of co-workers if they fail to do so.

It's better for Dogs to think carefully before they make any promises this month.

Although Dogs will have better luck in investments this month, they must be more conservative in handling their financial affairs. Otherwise they will lose a lot of money, not only in this month but also in the months to come. Under these circumstances it's better for Dogs try to keep to a tight budget at this stage.

Dogs should try to stop fooling around with several lovers at the same time during this period, because this will only bring endless trouble throughout the year.

The Third Month (5 April – 5 May)

A bad penny always turns up

This will be one of the most unfavourable months of the year for Dogs. There will be numerous difficulties and personal disputes at work. Dogs will be certain losers if they can't handle these matters properly from the very beginning. Their situation will be much better if Dogs are able to keep things under control as soon as possible.

Dogs should face their opponents with confidence and determination, otherwise they will be badly beaten. Someone may be watching them closely; Dogs must keep alert to prevent attacks from behind. Their jobs might be jeopardized if Dogs fail to do so. Apart from this, Dogs must watch for copycats carefully, or their profits will be taken away from them.

This is definitely not a profitable month for Dogs, so they must not try their luck at investments or gambling, or they will lose much more money than they ever anticipated.

A stranger may try to step in between Dogs and their lovers this month. Dogs should take this seriously or they will be very sorry about it sooner or later.

The Fourth Month (6 May – 5 June)

You can't get blood from a stone

Although there will be fewer difficulties and personal disputes at work this month, Dogs shouldn't lose concentration yet, or they might fall into business or money traps as a result. Keen perception is very important to Dogs, or they will be easily cheated.

Dogs should not talk too much about their future plans, and should try to hide their weaknesses from opponents this month – they will save themselves a lot of unnecessary trouble by doing so. One thing that Dogs must bear in mind is that they should try to be more independent and not rely too much on others at work. They will be turned down again and again when they ask for help.

Dogs won't have too much luck in love affairs this month. If they have been rejected several times, they should not ask for any favours for the time being, because all their efforts will be in vain.

The health of Dogs will begin to trouble them this month, so they should take good care of themselves. It's better for them to take a break or vacation to refresh themselves. Dogs should forget about any investments or gambling during this period of time.

The Fifth Month (6 June – 6 July)

All things come to those who wait

This is one of the most favourable months of the year for Dogs, in different ways. Dogs will finally have a chance of promotion during this period of time if they have really tried very hard at work in previous months. There will be room at the top for Dogs, but they shouldn't be hasty climbers or they will suffer from a sudden big fall. If they are patient enough, Dogs will be able to climb to the top without too much difficulty at the end of this month. Apart from this, Dogs must keep in mind that they should let other people talk first, and then they should wait for a suitable moment to express themselves clearly and properly. Dogs will become sure winners in any bargaining and negotiations during this period of time.

In money affairs, if Dogs can wait for a good time for their investments patiently, they will be able to receive handsome rewards in the very near future. Dogs will be quite fortunate in gambling in the middle of the month, but they should not be too greedy.

This month will be a very good time for Dogs to show their care and tenderness to their lovers. They will get a nice surprise in return by doing so. However, Dogs should not indulge themselves too much in entertainments this month.

The Sixth Month (7 July – 7 August)

Anger is a brief madness

The luck of Dogs will drop sharply this month, so they should be more cautious in handling their business. Dogs should double-check their work and documents during this period to make sure

---

that there are no careless mistakes, or they will have to learn a costly lesson. Most important of all, Dogs must try to calm themselves down and never let their temper get out of control. Because of the appearance of the Unlucky Star 'Five Ghosts' within the Sign, Dogs will be quite emotional and irrational this month, so it's necessary for them to keep calm for the time being, or their anger will ruin their careers totally. If they find that their temper is getting out of control, Dogs should try to walk away for a while, and then come back with a cool head.

Dogs must try not to risk their hard-earned money in any investments or gambling, or they will be very sorry in the months to come. If possible, Dogs should try their best to pay their bills as soon as possible within the month.

Dogs will easily get mad about their lovers, and that will seriously hurt their relationship. They should not be reluctant to say sorry to their lovers after their anger is all over.

The Seventh Month (8 August – 7 September)

Comparisons are odious

After the storm, there comes a calm. This month will be a peaceful period of time for Dogs at work. Their heavy workloads will be much relieved, and it's the time for Dogs to think about their future plans. But, first of all, Dogs should try to make an objective self-evaluation of themselves. It will be very helpful to their future development if Dogs are able to identify their weaknesses and try to do something about them at this stage.

However, Dogs should not try to compare their achievements with those of their competitors; this would be meaningless and unfair. Dogs will just confuse themselves by doing so.

It would also be ridiculous for Dogs to compare their lover with anyone else. This will only bring unnecessary trouble. Probably, their lover will walk away from them if they know anything about this.

The health of Dogs will be much improved this month, but they must watch their personal safety when engaged in outdoor activities. They should never risk their life just to satisfy a curiosity during this period.

The Eighth Month (8 September – 7 October)

Constant dripping wears away a stone

All of a sudden, bad luck will come back to Dogs as swiftly as a thunderstorm this month. Dogs must know how to protect themselves against this storm, or they will be eliminated. It's very important to hide in a safe place during a storm, so Dogs must keep a low profile and try not to expose themselves. If Dogs draw too much attention to themselves during this period, they will become a target for attack. If possible, Dogs should try to take a break or vacation for a short while to relax themselves. Being under the continuous tension brought on by a heavy workload may lead Dogs to suffer a nervous breakdown if they fail to find ways to relax properly. If anything goes wrong with them mentally, Dogs must go to see a therapist for treatment at once.

This is definitely not a profitable month for Dogs, so they must watch their money and valuables carefully. It's necessary for them to lock their windows and doors securely to avoid a possible burglary or a break-in in the middle of the month.

Dogs will be quite weak physically and mentally. Unless they can get enough rest and sleep, there will be a sudden collapse, and they will be probably hospitalized.

The Ninth Month (8 October – 6 November)

Good seeds make a good crop

Although Dogs have much better luck at work this month, they should not work too hard to avoid health problems. It would be a very good idea for Dogs to keep to a supervisory role at work, and let others handle the practical details for them.

There will be several opportunities knocking at their doors, and Dogs must know how to choose the proper one as their main target in the months to come. They will be very productive and successful if they are able to choose the right target, because only good seeds will make a good crop. The story will be quite different if they fail to do so.

Dogs will have pretty good luck in money affairs this month. Their income will come from different sources during this period of time, and will double. But they must not gamble away their hard-earned cash in the first 10 days of the month, or they will lose it.

Dogs may have to make a very important decision in love affairs this month. They should take it seriously, and try to think it over and over again. If possible, Dogs should ask advice from their parents or friends before they come to any decision.

The Tenth Month (7 November – 6 December)

Enough is as good as a feast

Greediness will bring destruction to Dogs, in both their business and financial affairs this month. Therefore, Dogs should try to content themselves with their present achievements. If they are too aggressive and too ambitious at work, Dogs will be isolated by their fellow workers and even their superiors. It will be much better if Dogs can keep in mind that 'Enough is as good as a feast.' Most important of all, Dogs should never try to challenge their superiors during this period, or their careers will be totally ruined as a result. They should keep their discontent in their hearts as a secret – a much safer way to go.

Although Dogs will be quite fortunate in money affairs this month, they should not be too greedy or they will only lose out in the end. As a matter of fact, Dogs will have nothing to worry about if they can remain satisfied with their present economic situation.

Dogs have to watch out carefully for the health and safety of younger family members this month. It's necessary for them to keep drugs and sharp objects, such as knives and scissors, out of reach of their children. If any accidents occur, Dogs must make sure their children get proper medical treatment at once.

The Eleventh Month (7 December – 5 January)

Hard work breaks no bones

There will be a very heavy workload waiting for Dogs this month, so they will have to put in extra time and effort. Although these challenges will be pretty tough, fortunately Dogs will be able to overcome most of them. It's necessary for Dogs to try their best to finish their jobs on time, no matter how difficult they are. Dogs should keep in mind that 'Hard work breaks no bones.' As a matter of fact, Dogs will be quite robust physically but will be pretty weak mentally this month. Therefore, Dogs must try to relax as much as they can to release the tensions. Dogs may have to travel a lot on business this month, but they should not complain too much about this as their efforts will be repaid handsomely sooner or later.

Dogs will lose a lot of money this month if they try their luck in investments or gambling. If they ask for a loan, they will be denied for sure. It's better for Dogs to keep as much cash as they can for unexpected expenses during this period of time.

This is definitely not a romantic month for Dogs. Their irrational behaviours may even scare their lover away from them.

However, this month will be a very good time for Dogs to spend more time with family members. Their children might be a very effective remedy for their tensions during this period.

The Twelfth Month (6 January – 3 February)

Knowledge is power

Although this hasn't be a very fortunate year for Dogs overall, they will see a successful end to it this month. They will become quite creative, and this will prove a great asset to their future development. This month will be a good time for Dogs to increase their knowledge by reading and studying, because they will be able to absorb different kinds of information and data easily during this period of time. The foundations of their business will be strengthened as a result. Dogs will be even more successful if they can find knowledgeable persons to consult about business matters. Apart from this, Dogs should be punctual for all appointments, and try to be well prepared, or they will miss out on several opportunities.

This will be a profitable month for Dogs. They will be able to gain handsome profits from different kinds of investments. But their luck in lotteries and gambling will be quite limited during this period of time.

Dogs will have a fresh start in their romance this month. They may get a second chance to mend a broken relationship. One thing Dogs should keep in mind is that they should never be reluctant to show their true feelings and care for their lover.

Using Feng Shui to Improve Fortune: Directions, Colours, Numbers and Lucky Charm

The ancient Chinese used the traditional Horoscope to predict their fortune on a yearly basis – they used the art of Feng Shui to improve their luck.

It was their belief that the application of tactical Feng Shui would change their bad luck into good, and make their good luck improve even more.

This same method is still effective in today's modern world.

There are four main elements which I will use in tactical Feng Shui:

◆ Lucky Directions
◆ Lucky Colours
◆ Lucky Numbers
◆ Lucky Charm

Dogs will have to put in extra time and effort at work this year, because they are going to have a very heavy workload. This will be a very busy year for them. Fortunately, their efforts won't be wasted because the more they work, the more they get. It won't be too difficult for Dogs to solve their business problems, but it will be quite difficult for them to settle personal conflicts and disputes with their colleagues. Apart from this, Dogs must respect the law and try not to get involved in anything illegal, or they will surely be punished or even put in gaol as a result. Although Dogs will have a steady regular income, they should never try to risk their money in investments or gambling during the year. If possible, Dogs must try to get enough rest and sleep, and take vacations to refresh themselves and avoid a possible nervous breakdown. Most important of all, Dogs must try to watch the health and safety of their children with extreme care.

Dogs will be quite popular sexually, but they should not try to fool around with several lovers at once or there will be endless trouble for them.

I would suggest applying the following Feng Shui tactics to improve luck so Dogs don't have to worry too much about their fate throughout the year.

Lucky Directions

The most favourable directions of the year for Dogs are **East**, **South** and **Northwest**. Dogs should sleep or sit in these directions if they wish to improve their fortune.

To make this procedure very simple, divide the house or room into nine imaginary squares. Then, using a compass, check the exact direction of each square as shown in Figure 5. This will help to ensure that you do not make a mistake with the direction.

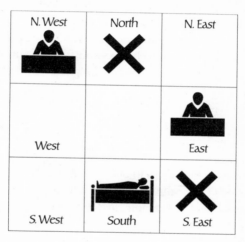

Figure 5

Dogs should sit in the East and Northwest at work or while studying; this will ensure that their achievements are much greater than the Stars intended. To improve health and achieve a good night's sleep, Dogs should position the bed in the favourable direction shown (South).

However, Dogs should try to keep away from the unfavourable directions of the year – that is, Southeast and North as shown in

Figure 5. Dogs should try not to sit, work or sleep in these directions, so as to get rid of the negative influences lurking there.

Lucky Colours

According to Chinese tradition, each of the five elements has its own representative colours. Fire is represented by red, pink and purple, Earth by yellow and brown, and so on. As a Feng Shui Master I would suggest **red**, **purple** and **white** as Dog's lucky colours for the year 2002.

Use these colours in paints, wall coverings, rugs, drapes and curtains. This will be sure to bring good fortune within the year.

However, Dogs should try not to use green or black in 2002, to avoid bad luck.

Lucky Numbers

The lucky numbers for Dogs in 2002 are: 3 and 9.

Fortune will be much improved by using these lucky numbers whenever possible. For example, if Dogs have a choice the phone number 239-3939 is better than 251-4411 – because the former contains more threes and nines, Dog's two lucky numbers for the year.

Lucky Charm

Feng Shui Masters believe that special objects can be used as a medium between human beings and nature. The fortune of the recipient is greatly improved as the positive wave of energy from nature is passed through the object or 'lucky charm' on to the recipient.

The lucky charm for the Dog in 2002 is a pair of magpies with peony flower on each of their backs. Magpies are considered to be a symbol of happiness while the peony is the symbol of richness. All together, this lucky charm means 'to be happy and rich'. For best results, it should be put in the northwest direction of the house.

豬

The

Pig

Years of the Pig

1911 (5/Feb/11—4/Feb/12)   1959 (4/Feb/59—4/Feb/60)
1923 (5/Feb/23—4/Feb/24)   1971 (4/Feb/71—4/Feb/72)
1935 (5/Feb/35—4/Feb/36)   1983 (4/Feb/83—3/Feb/84)
1947 (4/Feb/47—4/Feb/48)   1995 (4/Feb/95—3/Feb/96)

If you have any doubt about the classification of the 12 animal signs, or the divisions of months and years, please refer to pages xiii–xiv.

Distribution of the Stars within the Sign for 2002

Lucky Star   Unlucky Stars

Lunar Virtue   Deadly Spell
              Robbery Threat
              Gradual Drain

Lucky Star
Lunar Virtue

Virtue was highly appreciated by Confucius. The ancient Chinese believed that virtue not only set a good example for others to follow, but also produced its own rewards. Lunar Virtue is the least important of the four 'Virtue' Stars in the Chinese Horoscope, but is especially favourable for women.

When this Star appears, people will have enhanced persuasive skills which can help them achieve important breakthroughs. The effectiveness of this Star is usually not strong enough to suppress the Unlucky Stars if there are too many of them appearing together within a Sign.

Unlucky Stars
Deadly Spell

In ancient times, Chinese magic spells were created through special symbols and characters written by Taoist priests in red ink or even blood. Based on this, the concept of five 'Magic Spell' Stars in the Chinese Horoscope developed.

The most serious Star of all is the 'Deadly Spell'. The ancient Chinese believed that shortly before a person's death the Ruler of Hell would send an invisible 'Deadly Spell' as a summons to the afterlife.

When this Star appears, people have to be very careful about their health and safety to avoid serious illness, injury or even death.

Robbery Threat

Bandits were a nightmare for the peaceful Chinese peasants scattered throughout the rural areas, which were not well protected by local forces. Their money, crops or even their lives were under continuous threat so that they had to try very hard to protect themselves or they would become helpless victims.

When this Star appears, people should try not to walk alone in the dark streets, and they also should make sure all their windows and doors are locked securely.

Gradual Drain

Farming has been the major source of income for Chinese peasants for centuries. Because water is essential for irrigation, it has come to symbolize wealth. Over the centuries, Chinese peasants have worked to prevent drainage from their cultivated lands.

When this Star appears people need to watch their expenditure and keep within their budget. They should also avoid risky investments and gambling, which could easily lead to financial ruin.

General Overview of the Year

Pigs will have a much better year in 2002 than they had in 2001. They should try to make practical future plans for themselves at the beginning of the year if they wish to have a productive and successful one. There will be several opportunities knocking on their doors one after another throughout the year; Pigs should not hesitate too much, otherwise these opportunities will slip away and never come back again.

Pigs will become quite persuasive this year, and this skill will help them to achieve important breakthroughs in business. They will become even more successful if they can keep a positive and optimistic attitude at work throughout the year. If necessary, Pigs should not be reluctant to ask for help from the people who really care about them. Having a good team behind them will make Pigs become invincible in their business battles during the year.

The fortune of Pigs in money affairs is fair (i.e., not too good and not too bad). As long as they are not too greedy about money, they should be satisfied. Moderation will be the key to their economic growth throughout the year. The appearance of the Unlucky Star 'Gradual Drain' indicates that Pigs must watch their expenses very carefully. If they cannot cut down on their extravagant habits, Pigs will surely have money problems sooner or later.

Pigs must take good care of themselves, and try not to exhaust themselves too much. The appearance of the 'Deadly Spell' Unlucky Star is a warning signal to Pigs to watch their health closely, or there will be endless health problems in the coming years. Apart from this, Pigs should try not to walk alone in the dark streets at night and to keep their doors and windows securely locked to avoid a possible robbery.

Pigs will be quite attractive to others this year. If they wish to show their care and tenderness towards their lovers, they will get a nice surprise in return. Generally speaking, this should be a very romantic year for Pigs.

Career   * * *
Money   * *
Health   *
Love   * * * *

* * * * = Very Fortunate/ * * * = Pretty Good/ * * = Fair/ * = Unsatisfactory

Career * * *

Pigs will be quite productive and successful this year if they can make practical business plans at the beginning of the year. Most important of all, Pigs should not hesitate to take chances during the year, or they will miss out on several opportunities.

Their persuasive bargaining power will help them to achieve important breakthroughs in business. Whenever necessary, Pigs should not be reluctant to ask for help from those people who really care about them. Pigs will have pretty good luck at work during the second, third, fifth, sixth, ninth and eleventh months. They should try to make good use of these times.

Money **

This won't be a particularly fortunate year in money affairs for Pigs. However, they won't have to worry too much about their income. Their major concern is to try to cut back on their extravagant habits or their money will drain away. Apart from this, Pigs should try not to be greedy about money, or their greediness will lead them to self-destruction. Pigs must watch their financial situation during the fourth, sixth, seventh, eighth, tenth and the last month of the year. They will have better luck in money affairs during the second, third, fifth, ninth and eleventh months, and they had better try to make good use of these months.

Health *

Because of the appearance of the Unlucky Star 'Deadly Spell' within their Sign, Pigs must watch their health and safety very carefully to avoid accidents or a sudden collapse in health. Apart from this, Pigs should try not to walk alone in the dark streets at night to avoid being hurt by street violence or theft. And they should keep their windows and doors securely locked to avoid a possible robbery or break-in.

Pigs must take good care of themselves physically and mentally during the third and tenth months. They must watch their road safety with extreme care during the fourth month. Better to show up late than never at all.

Love ****

Pigs will be quite popular sexually, and they will have a very romantic year. If they wish to show their care and tenderness towards their lovers, Pigs will get a nice surprise in return. However, they will have some trouble in love affairs during the sixth and eighth months. Pigs should try to do something to improve their relationships with their lovers during these two months. Apart from this, Pigs will be quite comfortable in their love affairs.

Monthly In-depth Forecasts
The First Month (4 February – 5 March)

A light heart lives long

Although this will be a much better year for Pigs than last year, they won't see a very good beginning to the first month. There will be numerous personal disputes and rumours around them; Pigs should keep a low profile and try to settle these disputes one by one, patiently. Any radical or irrational action taken during this period of time will make the situation even worse. Pigs should keep in mind that 'A light heart lives long.'

If Pigs can maintain a positive and optimistic attitude, they will be much delighted by both their business and private life. Forgiveness will be a very effective tool for them at this time.

On the other hand, Pigs will be isolated and expelled by others in their business circle if they are too aggressive and ambitious at work.

This will be a romantic month for Pigs. They will be quite popular, but should not over-indulge in sex or alcohol, or their health will be destroyed. Moderation in all things will keep Pigs happy and healthy this month.

The fortune of Pigs in money affairs will be pretty good during the last 10 days of the month. Before that, they won't have too much luck in either investments or gambling.

The Second Month (6 March – 4 April)

Faith is the prerequisite to success

The luck of Pigs will be much improved this month, so they should try to make good use of this period of time. They will become quite creative and energetic this month, and these qualities will be important to their success at work. Most important of all, Pigs should try to keep faith in their business. All their efforts may be totally wasted if they fail to do so. As long as Pigs can keep in mind that 'Faith is the prerequisite to success,' they will be a sure winner in their career.

This month will be a very good time for Pigs to reach a mutual understanding and respect with their clients and co-workers. They will be the beneficiaries of this. Pigs should try to encourage mutual trust with their lovers during this period if they wish to improve and solidify their relationships. One thing that Pigs must keep in mind is that overdoing things will seriously hurt them, physically and mentally.

This will be a profitable month for Pigs, and there will be extra income from different sources. However, Pigs should try to cut back on their extravagant habits, or they will suffer financial difficulties in the months to come.

The Third Month (5 April – 5 May)

There is always a first time

Although Pigs will encounter some obstacles on their way to success this month, they will be able to overcome most of them if they have the guts to face them. As long as Pigs can keep their confidence and determination at work, they will create miracles in their business during this period of time. Most important of all, Pigs should not be shy about making necessary changes in business. Once they have started their new procedures, everything will be in proper order and they will have nothing to worry about. Pigs will be left far behind in the months to come if they refuse to make the necessary changes at this stage.

Pigs will still have luck in investments during this month. But they must keep their eyes wide open to money traps, or they will lose a lot of cash. They will also be easily cheated if they are too greedy about money.

The health of Pigs won't be too good this month; they must try to take especially good care of themselves. They must also try to get as much rest and sleep as they can at the end of the month, to avoid a collapse in health.

The Fourth Month (6 May – 5 June)

When the cat's away, the mice will play

This will be one of the most unfavourable months of the year for Pigs. They must prepare themselves for the unexpected during this period of time. For instance, contracts might be suddenly cancelled, proposals suddenly rejected, negotiations suddenly terminated and so on – Pigs must try their best to handle these kinds of problems carefully, and in person. The situation will become even worse if they rely on other people to take responsibility for them. It's necessary for Pigs to stay at their post this month, or their business will suffer during their absence. In other words, Pigs shouldn't try to take a break or vacation, or even a long business trip, at this critical moment.

This is definitely not a fortunate month for Pigs, and they will become the sure loser if they risk their hard-earned money in investments or gambling. If somebody invites them along on a joint business venture, Pigs should simply say no because this will save them from losing money in the months to come.

Pigs must watch their road safety very carefully this month, and their water safety as well. It's better to be safe than sorry.

This month won't be a romantic period of time for Pigs.

The Fifth Month (6 June – 6 July)

You can't win them all

Pigs will have much better luck at work this month. They will be very productive during this period of time if they keep working hard towards their career goals. Their outstanding performance will be greatly admired and appreciated by the people in their business circle.

Several invitations and offers will be waiting for them to choose between, as a result. It's up to Pigs to make their own choices. However, they should not be too ambitious, because it will be impossible to win them all. Just as the motto says, 'A bird in the hand is worth two in the bush.' Pigs will probably end up with nothing in hand if they are too greedy.

The same can be said of their private life. Their relationships with their lovers will be much improved if they are content with what they've got.

Although Pigs will be quite fortunate in their money affairs, they must try to keep to a tight budget or they will have financial difficulties in the near future.

Fortunately, the health of Pigs will be much improved this month.

The Sixth Month (7 July – 7 August)

A new broom sweeps clean

This will be one of the most favourable months of the year for Pigs, as long as they don't fool around – if they do, they will lose several opportunities during this period of time. Pigs might be promoted to a new position this month if they work hard enough, and they must try their best to make several necessary changes at this beginning stage. It will be impossible for them to improve their business later on if they fail to do so during this month. Pigs will be even more successful if they can win the support of colleagues during this period of time.

This month Pigs will spend much more money than anticipated; they must try to mind their expenses this month. It's necessary for them to pay bills as soon as possible, or they will be in deep trouble sooner or later.

Pigs should try not to show off too much this month, or they will be isolated by their friends. In love affairs they will feel quite lonely even though they will be surrounded by admirers. They shouldn't fret, it's just that there's nothing they can do about this state of affairs for the time being.

The Seventh Month (8 August – 7 September)

A bad workman blames his tools

All of a sudden bad luck will come as swiftly as a thunderstorm to Pigs this month. They'll have to struggle very hard for their survival in business, or they will be eliminated sooner or later. It's important for Pigs to take responsibility for their work, and not blame others for their failures. They will lose the respect and support of colleagues and subordinates if they refuse to accept responsibility for their own failures.

The best thing for Pigs to do at this critical moment is try to think of some alternative ways to correct their mistakes. Apart from this, Pigs must try to keep their eyes wide open to watch for hidden enemies around them and to prevent attacks from behind.

Pigs have to take good care of elderly family members at home. If anything goes wrong with them, Pigs must try to take them to the doctor or hospital for proper medical treatment at once. Any delay will be very dangerous.

This month is definitely not a fortunate period of time for Pigs. They may face financial difficulties if they can't keep to a tight budget.

The Eighth Month (8 September – 7 October)

Nothing will come of nothing

The luck of Pigs won't see too much improvement this month. This means, they will still suffer under the pressure of a heavy workload, just like last month. It's necessary for them to put in extra time and effort at work in order to survive. Pigs should not complain too much about their heavy workload, though, because they won't gain anything without sweat. They should keep in mind that their hard struggles at this stage will bring forth splendid achievements in the months to come. Pigs should try to improve business relations with their clients through direct personal contact. Their future development will be very successful if they are able to do this now.

Pigs will become quite emotional in their private life this month. Unless they can calm down, they will scare their friends and lovers away from them. If possible, Pigs should take a break or vacation at the end of the month.

Pigs must watch their money and valuables carefully to avoid theft. Because their fortune will be going up and down like a roller-coaster, Pigs should not try their luck in high-risk investments or gambling.

The Ninth Month (8 October – 6 November)

Unity is strength

Pigs will have much better luck at work this month. They must try their best to handle their daily work efficiently if they wish to see splendid achievements at the year end. Their diligence will help them to overcome most of their difficulties in business. But their success will be quite limited if they try to struggle on all alone. Pigs will be more productive if they form a strong and effective alliance with like-minded people. Just as the motto says, 'Unity is strength.' Teamwork will be the most effective means to future development. But Pigs have to realize that it will be more difficult to maintain an alliance than to organize one – they should consider this carefully at this beginning stage.

This will be a profitable month for Pigs. If they wish to buy valuables or property, Pigs should do it now. Pigs will have better luck in investments and gambling in the middle of the month.

Pigs will be quite popular sexually. This will be a romantic month for them. But they should try to be humble enough to avoid jealousy, or they will be isolated not only in this month, but also for the months to come.

The Tenth Month (7 November – 6 December)

Threatened men live long

This will be the last unfavourable month of the year for Pigs. They should try their best to pass this last severe test at work. Although Pigs will suffer from stress very much at work, they must try to keep their determination and confidence under any circumstances.

Just as the motto says, 'Threatened men live long.' Pigs will still be alive even after this critical moment. It will help Pigs a lot in their future development if they can take the experiences of this period as a valuable lesson. Their chance of survival in business will depend mainly on their ability to maintain an effective alliance. Apart from this, Pigs must not talk too much about their future plans, or there will be much unnecessary trouble in the near future.

Pigs must keep in mind that they should not try their luck in gambling, especially during the first 10 days of the month. It's necessary for Pigs to check if there are any leaks in their present accounting systems, and if there are they must try to do something about them as soon as possible.

It's necessary for Pigs to watch their diets and hygiene carefully this month, or they will suffer from infections. Apart from this, Pigs should try to get as much rest as they can to avoid physical exhaustion.

The Eleventh Month (7 December – 5 January)

Time and tide wait for no man

There will be several opportunities knocking at the door this month, and Pigs must try their best to seize some of them before they slip through their fingers. If they are too hesitant, Pigs will be very sorry to find out that these opportunities will never come back to them again. Just as the motto says, 'Time and tide wait for no man.' Pigs should take action fast as soon as opportunities appear. If somebody invites them to take part in a joint venture this month, Pigs should think about it carefully because it may very well prove profitable in the future.

This month will be a very good time for Pigs to carry out new projects because there will be fewer obstacles at this beginning stage. If they want to change jobs, Pigs should do it now.

This will be a profitable month for Pigs. They should think about investing their money in joint ventures during this period of time. They will have some luck in lottery and gambling this month, but they should be more conservative at the end of the month.

This month will be a very good time for Pigs to show their care and tenderness towards their lovers. They will have a nice surprise if they do so. They will miss a very good chance in love affairs if they are too shy to show their true feelings.

The Twelfth Month (6 January – 3 February)

One step at a time

Although Pigs won't have the same good luck at work this month as last month, they will see satisfactory achievements if they are not too aggressive. It will be much better for Pigs to be more conservative in handling their daily work during this period of time. This means that Pigs should try to carry out their business step by step, and never try to rush if they want to avoid a sudden big fall in their business. Moderation will be the key to business success at this stage. Any radical action will hurt the stability of their business seriously. Apart from this, Pigs must try not to challenge or to criticize their superiors, or their job will be jeopardized.

The fortunes of Pigs in money affairs will fluctuate this month; they should watch their investments carefully. Most important of all, Pigs have to watch out for money traps or they will be in big trouble.

This will be a romantic month for Pigs. However, they must try to keep away from alcohol and drugs during this period of time to ensure their health and safety.

Using Feng Shui to Improve Fortune: Directions, Colours, Numbers and Lucky Charm

The ancient Chinese used the traditional Horoscope to predict their fortune on a yearly basis – they used the art of Feng Shui to improve their luck.

It was their belief that the application of tactical Feng Shui would change their bad luck into good, and make their good luck improve even more.

This same method is still effective in today's modern world.

There are four main elements which I will use in tactical Feng Shui:

◆ Lucky Directions
◆ Lucky Colours
◆ Lucky Numbers
◆ Lucky Charm

Pigs will have a much better year in 2002 when compared with last year. There will be several opportunities knocking at their doors one after another throughout the year, but Pigs should try not to be too hesitant or the opportunities will slip away and never come back again. Pigs will be quite skilful at bargaining; they should therefore try to make good use of their persuasive powers during the year. They will become even more successful if they can keep a positive and optimistic attitude at work. Having a good team of dependable partners will make Pigs invincible in their business battles.

If Pigs are not too greedy about money, their financial situation will be quite satisfactory this year. However, they must watch their expenses to avoid money problems.

Pigs should try not to exhaust themselves too much at work, or they will suffer from endless health problems in the coming years. In love affairs, Pigs will become quite popular, and if they show care and tenderness to their lovers they will get a nice surprise in return.

I would suggest applying the following Feng Shui tactics to ensure greater success throughout the year.

Lucky Directions

The most favourable directions of the year for Pigs are **East**, **Southwest** and **West**. Pigs should sleep or sit in these directions if they wish to improve their fortune.

To make this procedure very simple, divide the house or room into nine imaginary squares. Then, using a compass, check the exact direction of each square as shown in Figure 6. This will help to ensure that you do not make a mistake with the direction.

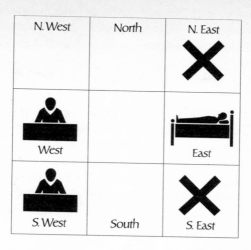

N. West	North	N. East
		✗
West		East
S. West	South	S. East
		✗

Figure 6

Pigs should sit in the Southwest and West at work or while studying; this will ensure that their achievements are much greater than the Stars intended. To improve health and achieve a good night's sleep, Pigs should position the bed in the favourable direction shown (East).

However, Pigs should try to keep away from the unfavourable directions of the year – that is, Southeast and Northeast, as shown in Figure 6. Pigs should try not to sit, work or sleep in these directions, so as to get rid of the negative influences lurking there.

Lucky Colours

According to Chinese tradition, each of the five elements has its own representative colours. Fire is represented by red, pink and purple, Earth by yellow and brown, and so on. As a Feng Shui Master I would suggest **blue**, **grey**, **yellow** and **brown** as Pig's lucky colours for the year 2002.

Use these colours in paints, wall coverings, rugs, drapes and curtains. This will be sure to bring good fortune within the year.

However, Pigs should try not to use white, orange or red in 2002, to avoid bad luck.

Lucky Numbers

The lucky numbers for Pigs in 2002 are: 2 and 3.

Fortune will be much improved by using these lucky numbers whenever possible. For example, if Pigs have a choice, the phone number 2334-3322 is better than 2876-4466 – because the former contains more twos and threes, Pig's two lucky numbers for the year.

Lucky Charm

Feng Shui Masters believe that special objects can be used as a medium between human beings and nature. The fortune of the recipient is greatly improved as the positive wave of energy from nature is passed through the object or 'lucky charm' on to the recipient.

The lucky charm for the Pig is a pair of dragon-head turtles climbing up a stone with a laurel branch in their mouths. In the olden days, only the first scholar who passed the nationwide civil examination was given the honour of standing near the dragon-head turtle statue inside the Emperor's hall. Eventually, the dragon-head turtle became the symbol of success in examinations with great promise. For best results, this lucky charm should be put in the southwest direction of the house.

Chapter Seven

The

Mouse

Years of the Mouse

1912 (5/Feb/12—3/Feb/13) 1960 (5/Feb/60—3/Feb/61)
1924 (5/Feb/24—3/Feb/25) 1972 (5/Feb/72—3/Feb/73)
1936 (5/Feb/36—3/Feb/37) 1984 (4/Feb/84—3/Feb/85)
1948 (5/Feb/48—3/Feb/49) 1996 (4/Feb/96—3/Feb/97)

If you have any doubt about the classification of the 12 animal signs, or the divisions of months and years, please refer to pages xiii–xiv.

Distribution of the Stars within the Sign for 2002

Lucky Stars **Unlucky Stars**

None   Heavenly Weeping
          Huge Drain
          Broken Down
          Iron Bars
          Conflict of the Year
          Disastrous Threat
          Gaol House

Unlucky Stars
Heavenly Weeping

The ancient Chinese believed that Heaven was capable of reacting to and being sensitive towards the experiences and plight of those on earth. If the people suffered from starvation and violence, then Heaven would weep for them. Thus, the appearance of 'Heavenly Weeping' indicates troubles.

When this Star appears, people will face a lot of problems and will have to struggle hard to get out from under them.

Huge Drain

The ancient Chinese considered water to be the symbol of wealth, since it was essential to agriculture, the backbone of their economy. On a farm, a failure to manage water could easily lead to dried-out crops, spelling disaster.

This Star's appearance is a warning that a large and sudden financial loss is on the horizon.

Broken Down

The ancient Chinese had little regard for objects that were not whole and/or contained cracks. In a similar way, a broken soul was much depreciated.

The appearance of this Star is a bad omen. People should watch out for their morals and conduct. At the same time, they should also try very hard to protect themselves from injury.

Iron Bars

In the Chinese Horoscope the Stars 'Iron Bars' and 'Gaol House' are similar to each other in that they both deal with confinement and punishment for a crime. However, 'Iron Bars' is not as serious as 'Gaol House', since the former refers to a place of temporary detention while the latter is more like a maximum-security prison.

When this Star appears, be careful not to break the law – or be prepared to suffer the consequences.

Conflict of the Year

Since the ancient Chinese valued harmony, they would try to minimize conflicts quickly, as soon as they broke out. Because this Star signifies conflict, it is not regarded as a good omen.

If this Star appears within a Sign, people have to try their best to settle all disputes and conflicts before they get out of hand. Otherwise they will face a lot of problems and their work will be handicapped as a result.

Disastrous Threat

This is one of the four 'Threat' Stars in the Chinese Horoscope. Its appearance is a serious warning to people that if they don't take precautions to protect themselves they could face disastrous results.

People should pay more attention to protect their houses as well as their own safety. They should try to keep away from dangers and try not to take any risks. 'Safety first' is the most important rule that they should follow within the year.

Gaol House

Going through the judicial system was often a nightmare for the ancient Chinese, since their human rights were not well protected by the judicial system. They would rather have died than have to go to prison.

When this Star appears, people will have a tendency to get in trouble with the law. It is best to stay on the straight and narrow and avoid anything that causes trouble. Keep in mind that 'it is better to be a hungry bird in the forest than a well-fed bird in a cage'.

General Overview of the Year

Because of the appearance of so many Unlucky Stars within their Sign, Mice will have a pretty tough year in 2002. They will face many problems in both their business and private life. It's very important for Mice to try to put in extra time and effort at work if they are to survive in business. The appearance of the 'Conflict of the Year' Star indicates that Mice must try to improve their relationships with clients and co-workers, or their job might be jeopardized. Most important of all, Mice must try to carry out their work legally without breaking any regulations, or they might end up in gaol.

Fortunately, their fate will be turning to a positive trend at the end of the year. Mice must try their best to survive and never give up during the first half of the year, or they won't be able to taste the sweetness of success in the last two months of the year.

Mice will become more and more sensitive to and critical of others, and that will bring about a lot of conflict with the people around them. It would be much better for Mice to concentrate on their own business and forget about other people's. They will be more happy and successful by doing so.

This is definitely not a profitable year for Mice, and they should try to be more conservative in handling their investments. Because of the appearance of the 'Huge Drain' Star, Mice must watch their expenses very closely and try to keep to a tight budget.

Mice must watch their personal safety carefully this year. They must try to keep away from heights to avoid a sudden big fall.

Mice won't have too much luck in love affairs this year. They should forget about their troubles and sorrows in love affairs, and concentrate more on their work throughout the year.

Career	★ ★
Money	★
Health	★ ★
Love	★

★ ★ = Fair/ ★ = Unsatisfactory

Career **

Mice will face numerous difficulties and disputes at work this year, so that it will be necessary for them to put in extra time and effort in handling their business if they don't want to be eliminated by the end of the year. Most important of all, Mice should try their best to improve relationships with clients and co-workers, and to settle conflicts as soon as possible, or their chance of survival in business will be seriously hurt. Good working relationships will help Mice a lot in their business development this year.

Mice should keep alert for the unexpected in business during the first, second, fifth, ninth and tenth months of the year. They will keep afloat if they can pass the severe tests of these months. However, Mice will have much better luck at work during the third, sixth, seventh and the last month of the year. If they can make good use of these four months they will find they can achieve a good deal.

Money *

Because of the appearance of the Unlucky Star 'Huge Drain' within their Sign, Mice won't have too much luck in money affairs this year. Therefore, Mice should not try their luck in high-risk investments or gambling, or they will be a sure loser. Most important of all, Mice should try to watch their expenses this year. Unless they can keep to a tight budget, Mice will have financial problems. It would be much better if Mice can save as much money as they can for the many unexpected expenses which will arise throughout the year. The most unfavourable months in money affairs for Mice will be the second, fourth, fifth, eighth, ninth and tenth months of the year. Mice must try to handle their money affairs most carefully during these months. However, the first, sixth, seventh and the last month of the year will be the most fortunate months of the year for Mice and their money.

Health * *

There won't be too many health problems for Mice this year, but they must guard their personal safety carefully. Because of the appearances of the Unlucky Stars 'Broken Down' and 'Disastrous Threat', Mice may face several injuries from accidents. They must try to take good care of themselves and try to keep away from danger. Most important of all, they must try to keep away from cliffs and high walls to avoid a heavy sudden fall. 'Safety first' is the most important rule they should follow within the year. Mice should pay most attention to their safety during the second, third, fourth, ninth and the last month of the year.

Love *

Mice will be quite active in love affairs, but they will not be very popular this year, and might be deeply disappointed as a result. However, Mice should not be frustrated if they have been turned down several times in love affairs, because next year their luck will change. Because of the appearance of the Unlucky Star 'Conflict of the Year', Mice will experience many conflicts with their friends and lovers. Mice should try to stay calm and settle these conflicts patiently and sincerely. Mice will have better luck in love affairs during the third and the last two months of the year.

Monthly In-depth Forecasts
The First Month (4 February – 5 March)

When in Rome, do as the Romans do

Mice have to prepare themselves to struggle hard for their business this year, or they will be badly defeated. Fortunately, they will have a pretty good start to the year. If Mice can make good use of this opportunity to equip themselves psychologically and financially, they will be in a much better position in the months to come. Mice should try to be more flexible to suit the circumstances in order to eliminate unnecessary trouble. They should keep in mind that, when in Rome, it's best to do as the Romans do.

The fortune of Mice will be pretty good during this period of time. They will have a satisfactory income from different sources, but they must watch out for pickpockets at weekends.

This won't be a romantic month for Mice. Due to their pride, Mice will try to hide their true feelings, so they will be somewhat misunderstood and isolated in their private life.

Mice should watch their diet closely, or they will suffer from digestive diseases.

The Second Month (6 March – 4 April)

If you play with fire you get burned

This is definitely not a good month for Mice. They will meet with a lot of problems at work; it will be necessary for them to handle these problems calmly but promptly before they get out of hand. However, if they can carry out their work according to the relevant regulations, there won't be too many problems. But if Mice try to break the law and play with fire, they will surely get burned.

Mice should try to seek professional advice from experts if they don't want to get involved in any legal battles. Apart from this, it's very important for Mice to go through all their contracts and documents very carefully, because any careless mistakes will prove costly.

Mice have to watch their road safety carefully. They should try to drive and walk as cautiously as they can, especially in the last 10 days of the month.

The fortune of Mice will be at a low ebb. They must not gamble their money in any high-risk investments. It's necessary for them to save money for the rainy days to come.

The Third Month (5 April – 5 May)

Thrift is a great revenue

The fortune of Mice will be much improved this month. The financial difficulties of last month will be somewhat dissolved, and Mice will be able to find some extra income from different sources. Mice will also receive handsome bonuses from various investments. Although they will have some luck in gambling, Mice should not be too greedy. No matter how lucky they are, Mice should try to save as much money as they can; otherwise their money will be easy come, easy go, and they will end up with nothing in hand as a result.

It's necessary for Mice to watch their property and valuables. Apart from this, they must keep their doors and safes securely locked to avoid burglary or robbery.

Mice have to watch their personal safety when in wild areas, and keep away from steep cliffs in order to avoid a sudden fall.

Mice will have much better luck in love affairs this month. They should try their best to show their true feelings to their loved ones, or they will miss a very good chance.

The Fourth Month (6 May – 5 June)

Better to be safe than sorry

The luck of Mice will slip a bit this month. The major concern for them during this period will be their personal safety, indoors and out. First of all, Mice must watch their step when they are walking up and down stairs. Apart from this, they should watch for falling objects too. Most important of all, they must try to keep far away from violent activities. It is better to be safe than sorry.

Mice will spend more money than anticipated this month, so they should try to keep to a tight budget and not let expenses get out of control. Otherwise they will be in deep trouble financially in the months to come. Gambling will gain them nothing but total destruction during this period of time.

Mice will be quite sentimental this month. Although they are longing for love and care, they will be deeply disappointed.

However, Mice should try to show their sincerity to the people around them to win their admiration and respect. Mice will be busily engaged in different social gatherings, and they should not be too cool to either new or old acquaintances.

The Fifth Month (6 June – 6 July)

It is no use crying over spilled milk

This will be one of the most unfavourable months of the year for Mice. They will suffer very much under the burden of a heavy workload. They'll have to work very hard just to survive. Even so, unfortunately all their efforts may probably be in vain. Mice may have to taste the bitterness of defeat during this period of time. If that really happens, Mice should not be too sorry, because it's no use crying over spilled milk. Mice should try to think about their recovery. Since they are going to have better luck in the next three months, it's better for Mice to start to get on with rebuilding as soon as possible.

Mice may face a broken relationship if they don't know how to take care of their loved ones. However, they should not be too sorry if a relationship fails, because they will have a new romance in a few months' time.

The fortune of Mice in money affairs will be terrible this month. They should never borrow any money from any source, or they will be in big trouble. Investments and gambling should be stopped temporarily if Mice don't want to suffer a big loss.

Fortunately, the Mouse's luck will change for the better towards the end of the month.

The Sixth Month (7 July – 7 August)

A change is as good as a rest

Mice will have some release from last month's heavy workload. Now, they can smell the fresh air after a thunderstorm.

What Mice should do now is to plan for their future development properly, so they can avoid big losses in the thunderstorms to come. Although this is definitely not a good year for Mice, if they know how to handle the situation they might still be able to have a satisfactory result at year end. Mice should be more aggressive at work when the time is right, and more conservative during unfavourable periods.

Mice should try to be more active in building up a better business relationship with their clients. Contact clients and understanding what they really want will be vital to their future business development. Apart from this, Mice should try to develop a new system, and not be bound by old custom and practice. Renovation is very important for their survival and continuous development in business.

Obviously, the fortune of Mice is changing for the better this month. Yet they still have to watch their expenses.

The love affairs of Mice will turn over a new leaf during this period.

The Seventh Month (8 August – 7 September)

God helps those who help themselves

This will be one of the most favourable months of the year for Mice. If Mice wish to end the year on a high note, they have to put more time and effort in business at this stage. Since they are going to have much better luck at work during this period, their rewards might be doubled or even tripled. Mice should realize that they have no one to rely upon but themselves. If Mice want to change their job, this month is the most suitable time.

Fortune in money affairs will still be quite good for Mice this month. If they want to invest their money in buying property or valuable items, this will be a very good time. Mice will also have some luck in gambling at the beginning of the month.

Mice have to watch their health or they will suffer from digestive and respiratory diseases. However, they will enjoy a very sweet romantic time with their loved ones.

The Eighth Month (8 September – 7 October)

Little leaks sink the ship

Again, the luck of Mice is going downhill this month. Although this is not a big thunderstorm, it is a heavy rain. This heavy rainfall will cause many little leaks, and the leaks will sink the ship. Mice must watch those small leakages in their business systems. If they don't try to repair them properly, their business will sink to the bottom of the sea. It's necessary for Mice to double-check their documents, contracts and accounts to make sure that they contain no careless mistakes, as these would prove costly.

Honesty is the best policy. Mice should not lie to their friends or lovers, especially during the latter half of this month. Mice will find that they are caught in a critical situation if they do. Instead, Mice should try to build up a mutual understanding with their friends and lovers during this period.

Fortune in money affairs will be going down sharply this month. Consequently, Mice should be more conservative in their investments. There may be some unexpected expenses at the end of the month.

The Ninth Month (8 October – 6 November)

Accidents will happen

This is one of the most unfavourable months of the year for Mice. Unless Mice are well prepared psychologically, they will be left high and dry, a helpless victim after the storm. Mice will face dramatic and drastic changes at work, and they'll have to adjust quickly to their new environment or they will be eliminated sooner or later. Worst of all, they may lose their leadership or partnership role all of a sudden. Mice may be able to keep these events from happening if they know how to settle personal disputes.

Mice must watch their safety when they go out on trips. It's necessary for them to keep away from dangerous places such as cliffs, the desert, volcanoes and the seashore. Apart from this, Mice should try to keep away from knives and pistols, too.

Mice have to be more conservative in money affairs. Their regular income may be endangered and there might be a shortage of cash for a period of time during this month. Mice should be well prepared for this critical situation.

The Tenth Month (7 November – 6 December)

Bad money drives out good

The fortune of Mice in money affairs will be at its lowest point this month. Their investments will be messed up, and it would be much better for them to stop all this kind of activity during this period. Apart from this, Mice must try to cut back on their extravagant tastes and habits, or they will be in deep financial trouble.

It's very important for Mice to forget about gambling for the time being.

Mice will face strong challenges at work. Some competitors may try to copy their ideas and take profits away from them. Unless Mice can do something to stop them, they may become helpless victims. However, Mice will be able to survive if they stand firm and refuse to give up.

Mice have to watch their love affairs carefully, because there may be a stranger trying to step in between their lovers and them. Things will become even more complicated if they don't pay enough attention to this matter.

The Eleventh Month (7 December – 5 January)

A bird never flew on one wing

Fortunately, the luck of Mice is going to change for the better this month. They will still be feeling the effects of last month's heavy burdens, however. That means they'll have to work hard for their survival in business, or they will be eliminated. The challenges from competitors will still threaten them, and their nightmares at work are not all over yet. What Mice should do now is try to organize a united force to fight back effectively. Mice will be defeated badly if they try to fight alone during this period. The result will be quite different if they can join forces with others. They should keep this motto in mind: 'A bird never flew on one wing.'

If Mice can build mutual understanding between themselves and their loved ones, any third party will surely be expelled very soon. But if they fail to do so, the story will be quite different.

Mice should try to get out from under the influence of wicked so-called friends, or they will be involved in legal problems. In addition, Mice should try not to break any laws for any reason, or they may end up facing a lawsuit, or even find themselves in gaol.

The Twelfth Month (6 January – 3 February)

Slowly but surely

Finally, Mice get some kind of release after long struggles. Their luck improves somewhat this month, 'Slowly but surely'. What Mice should do at this stage is try to build good business and personal relationships for their future development in the year to come. Apart from this, they should try to relax a little bit to avoid over-exhaustion. Mice should try not to be too aggressive right at the beginning, and try to be more co-operative towards their partners.

The fortune in money affairs will be fully recovered during this period of time, so Mice will be able to gain profits from their various investments. And they will have extra income from different sources. However, Mice have to watch out for pickpockets when they go out at night.

Although Mice will be in pretty good shape this month, they will be easily hurt by sharp objects. Therefore, they must try to keep away from knives, saws, axes and so on.

Fortunately, their relationship with their loved ones will be in a pretty stable condition.

Using Feng Shui to Improve Fortune: Directions, Colours, Numbers and Lucky Charm

The ancient Chinese used the traditional Horoscope to predict their fortune on a yearly basis – they used the art of Feng Shui to improve their luck.

It was their belief that the application of tactical Feng Shui would change their bad luck into good, and make their good luck improve even more.

This same method is still effective in today's modern world.

There are four main elements which I will use in tactical Feng Shui:

- ◆ Lucky Directions
- ◆ Lucky Colours
- ◆ Lucky Numbers
- ◆ Lucky Charm

Mice will have to put in more time and effort at work because they are going to have a pretty tough year in 2002. They should keep their eyes wide open to watch for possible dangers, or they will suffer from a sudden collapse in business. If they are able to settle most of the conflicts at work, Mice will have a better chance to survive to the end of the year. Most important of all, Mice should never try to break any regulations or laws during the year, or they will be severely punished.

This is definitely not a profitable year for Mice, and they must try to be more conservative in handling their investments. Unless they can try to keep to a tight budget, their money will drain away from them very rapidly.

Mice need not to worry about their health, but they must watch their personal safety carefully. It would be much better if Mice were to try to keep away from dangerous heights to avoid a sudden big fall.

Unfortunately, Mice won't have too much luck in love affairs this year. They should forget about their sorrows in love affairs and concentrate more on their work.

I would suggest applying the following Feng Shui tactics to improve luck so that Mice don't have to worry too much about their fate within the year.

Lucky Directions

The most favourable directions of the year for Mice are **Southeast**, **Southwest** and **Northeast**. Mice should sleep or sit in these directions if they wish to improve their fortune.

To make this procedure very simple, divide the house or room into nine imaginary squares. Then, using a compass, check the exact direction of each square as shown in Figure 7. This will help to ensure that you do not make a mistake with the direction.

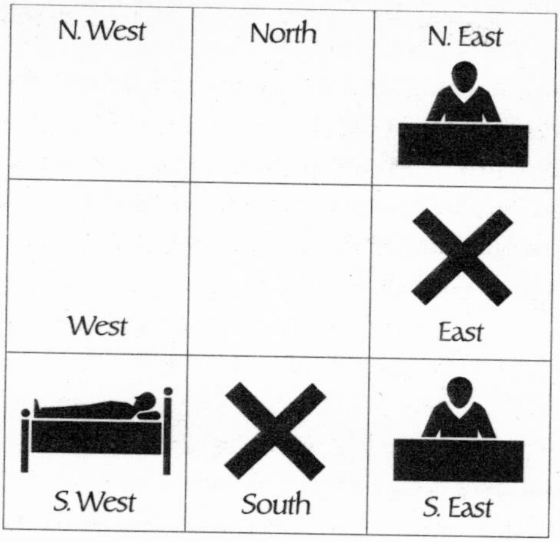

N. West	North	N. East
West		East
S. West	South	S. East

Figure 7

Mice should sit in the Southeast and Northeast at work or while studying; this will ensure that their achievements are much greater than the Stars intended. To improve health and achieve a good night's sleep, Mice should position the bed in the favourable direction shown (Southwest).

However, Mice should try to keep away from the unfavourable directions of the year – that is, East and South, as shown in Figure 7. Mice should try not to sit, work or sleep in these directions, so as to get rid of the negative influences lurking there.

Lucky Colours

According to Chinese tradition, each of the five elements has its own representative colours. Fire is represented by red, pink and purple, Earth by yellow and brown, and so on. As a Feng Shui Master I would suggest **green**, **yellow** and **brown** as the Mouse's lucky colours for the year 2002.

Use these colours in paints, wall coverings, rugs, drapes and curtains. This will be sure to bring good fortune within the year.

However, Mice should not use red, purple or white in 2002, to avoid bad luck.

Lucky Numbers

The lucky numbers for Mice in 2002 are: **3** and **6**.

Fortune will be much improved by using these lucky numbers whenever possible. For example, if Mice have a choice, the phone number 2336-6633 is better than 2553-8822 – because the former contains more threes and sixes, the Mouse's two lucky numbers for the year.

Lucky Charm

Feng Shui Masters believe that special objects can be used as a medium between human beings and nature. The fortune of the recipient is greatly improved as the positive wave of energy from nature is passed through the object or 'lucky charm' on to the recipient.

The lucky charm for the Mouse in 2002 is a monkey and a dragon, each with a gourd. With the help of monkey and dragon, the Mouse will be able to survive even though they will have serious conflicts in the year of the Horse. Gourds are generally regarded as the symbol of good medical care, in other words good health. For best results, this lucky charm should be put in the northeast direction of the house.

Chapter Eight

The

Ox

Years of the Ox

1913 (4/Feb/13—3/Feb/14)	1961 (4/Feb/61—3/Feb/62)
1925 (4/Feb/25—3/Feb/26)	1973 (4/Feb/73—3/Feb/74)
1937 (4/Feb/37—3/Feb/38)	1985 (4/Feb/85—3/Feb/86)
1949 (4/Feb/49—3/Feb/50)	1997 (4/Feb/97—3/Feb/98)

If you have any doubt about the classification of the 12 animal signs, or the divisions of months and years, please refer to pages xiii–xiv.

Distribution of the Stars within the Sign for 2002

Lucky Stars   Unlucky Stars

Lucky Stars	Unlucky Stars
Dragon's Virtue	Heavenly Threat
Crape Myrtle	Heavenly Hazards
	Yearly Threat
	Sudden Collapse

Lucky Stars
Dragon's Virtue

Virtue was highly appreciated by Confucius. The ancient Chinese believed that virtue not only set a good example to others, but provided its own good results. Of the four 'Virtue' Stars in the Chinese Horoscope, 'Dragon's Virtue' is one of the most important.

Since for centuries the dragon was regarded as a symbol of the Emperor, the 'Dragon's Virtue' signified the Emperor's virtue and goodness, which would benefit the entire empire and its people.

When this Star appears, people will have a successful and productive year. They will get support from other people, especially their subordinates.

Crape Myrtle

Since the flower Crape Myrtle was deliberately planted inside the royal courts of the Forbidden City, it became known as the Emperor's flower. Later, it came to symbolize superiority within the feudal hierarchy.

People under this Star will easily get major promotions, and will have the authority and confidence to overcome all difficulties and opposition they may face.

Unlucky Stars
Heavenly Threat

The ancient Chinese believed that malevolent spirits brought dangers and problems into their daily lives. Of these, 'Heavenly Threat' was considered to be the most dangerous of all, and able to cause serious damage.

The appearance of this Star is a warning to be more careful. Watch out for potential dangers and traps. Follow a conservative, defensive strategy.

Heavenly Hazards

The ancient Chinese believed that the gods in heaven would deliberately confront people with difficult obstacles in life to test them. Those who failed to pass these dangerous tests, it was believed, would be given a miserable life. Not surprisingly, this Star is considered a bad omen.

When this Star appears, people will face many challenges, which they must overcome if they want to avoid losing out.

Yearly Threat

The ancient Chinese believed that malevolent spirits brought dangers and problems into their daily lives. The Star 'Yearly Threat' was one of these. Its appearance is a bad omen.

When this Star appears, people need to improve relations with others, especially with lovers and spouses, to avoid endless arguments and quarrels.

Sudden Collapse

A building, project or business will ultimately collapse if it lacks a solid foundation – one which must be steadily maintained. 'Sudden Collapse', as its name suggests, is considered to be a bad omen. In order to prevent this kind of tragedy, people have to build up their foundation slowly but surely.

When this Star appears within a Sign, people have to watch out for the economic growth of their business, and for sudden changes such as a dramatic drop in sales and production or cancellation of contracts, etc.

General Overview of the Year

Because of the appearances of the two Lucky Stars 'Dragon's Virtue' and 'Crape Myrtle' within their Sign, Oxen will have a pretty productive and successful year in 2002. Their creativity will bring forth splendid achievements to them if they really try hard enough for their careers. However, Oxen should not be blinded by their successes, or they might face a sudden collapse in their business. It's necessary for Oxen to try to keep a low profile after their successes to avoid unnecessary trouble from jealous people around them. In other words, Oxen should try to be aggressive in their business, but try to be humble and conservative in handling personal affairs. The appearance of the Unlucky Star 'Heavenly Threat' indicates that Oxen must watch out very carefully for potential dangers and traps in business.

Fortunately, Oxen will be able to handle almost all these dangers if they are focused and not fooling around at work. This year, Oxen will have satisfactory income from different sources. However, this won't be a very profitable year for them, so that it will be much better if Oxen are more conservative in their investments to avoid a sudden collapse in money affairs. Apart from this, Oxen must watch the economic growth of their business closely, to catch sudden changes such as a dramatic drop in sales and production or cancellation of contracts, etc.

Fortunately, Oxen will be quite healthy this year. However, they should watch their diet to avoid food poisoning and infections. Most important of all, Oxen must watch their personal safety with extreme care when engaged in outdoor activities.

This is definitely not a romantic year for Oxen. They should take it easy and try not to bury themselves in deep sorrow over a broken relationship. If they can reach a mutual understanding with their lovers, the situation will be much improved.

Career   ★ ★ ★ ★
Money   ★ ★
Health   ★ ★
Love   ★

★ ★ ★ ★ = Very Fortunate/★ ★ = Fair/★ = Unsatisfactory

Career ****

Oxen will be quite productive and successful at work this year if they work hard enough. They may be promoted as a result of their outstanding performance. However, Oxen should not be blinded by their success, or they will face a tremendous defeat sooner or later. Their major concern of the year is how to maintain or improve their business relationships with colleagues and clients. Oxen will become even more successful if they are able to do so. Oxen will have pretty good luck at work during the first, second, fourth, seventh, eighth and the last two months of the year. But they should pay more attention to settling difficulties in their business during the third, sixth, ninth and tenth months.

Money **

Although this won't be a very profitable year for Oxen, they will be able to earn a satisfactory income from different sources. One thing Oxen should keep in mind is that they should try not to risk their hard-earned money in investments and gambling. They will be much happier if they are not too greedy in money affairs. Oxen will be more fortunate in money affairs during the first, second, fourth, eighth and eleventh months of the year. Their major concern is to try to save money for unexpected expenses throughout the year.

Health **

Generally speaking, Oxen will be quite healthy throughout the year. The only thing they have to worry about is their diet. It will be much better if Oxen can keep away from raw foods, or they might suffer from food poisoning. Other than that, Oxen will be quite all right physically and mentally. However, it's necessary for Oxen to watch their safety when engaged in outdoor activities.

Oxen must watch out for possible danger during the second, third, sixth, ninth and the last month of the year. Most important of all, Oxen must take extreme care of their children during the second month, and drive very carefully during the third and seventh months of the year.

Love *

This is definitely not a romantic year for Oxen. No matter how hard they try to impress, they just have no luck in love affairs during the year. Their situation will become even worse if they try to cheat their lovers. They might face a broken relationship by doing that in the latter part of the year. They should keep in mind that 'Honesty is the best policy' in their love affairs.

Oxen will have better luck in love affairs during the first, fifth and eleventh months of the year. If Oxen are able the reach a mutual understanding and trust with their lovers, their situation will be much improved.

Monthly In-depth Forecasts
The First Month (4 February – 5 March)

Every man is the architect of his own fortune

Oxen will have a very successful and productive year in 2002 if they work hard enough. They are going to have a very good start to the beginning of the year. Chances will come knocking at their doors one after another, and they should try to keep alert and don't let these opportunities slip through their fingers. It's all up to Oxen to determine how successful they will be this year – they are the architects of their own fortune. Although diligence is essential to their success, good planning is also very important. It's necessary for Oxen to have a clever strategy, and carry it out step by step if they want to see important career breakthroughs at year end.

Oxen will have some luck in gambling and lucky draws, but they should not be too greedy. Their investments will bring profits to them during this period. If Oxen are asking for a loan, they will be easily approved.

This month Oxen will enjoy a sweet relationship with their loved ones, but they should not spend too much time in love affairs. At least they should try not to mix their business life with their private life. They should be fully aware that they must put work before pleasure.

The Second Month (6 March – 4 April)

As you begin, so shall you proceed

Oxen have to take action during this period. Hopefully they will have planned their strategy last month; now it's the time for them to take their first step. Oxen should not be too hesitant about starting a new project, or they will miss a very good chance. Once they start, everything will be ready for them. Even though Oxen may have some minor problems at the beginning, these will be settled easily sooner or later. Simply speaking, Oxen must have the guts to start a new project or even a new job.

Although their fortune in money affairs will be going down a little bit this month, Oxen don't have to worry about their finances. They will have a steady income, and their luck in gambling is still pretty good.

Oxen have to watch the safety and health of younger family members. They must take them to the doctors to have proper medical treatment as soon as possible. Apart from this, Oxen should be alert to the danger of fire at home near the end of the month.

The Third Month (5 April – 5 May)

United we stand, divided we fall

This is one of the most unfavourable months of the year for Oxen. They will face numerous difficulties in their daily work, and this could threaten their jobs if they can't handle them properly. Apart from this, personal conflicts and disputes will keep on bothering them from time to time. So, first of all it's necessary for Oxen to build up a better relationship with co-workers in order to eliminate the unnecessary personal disputes and misunderstandings in the office. Then, Oxen should try to form an alliance with the people around them to fight for their rights. Oxen will be in a very good position if they are able to do so.

Collective bargaining can help Oxen to overcome obstacles in business during the month. They will be pretty weak in front of their opponents if they fail to do so.

Oxen have to drive very carefully this month. Again, they should watch out for fire both at home and at work.

The fortune in money affairs of Oxen will fluctuate from time to time. It would be wise for them not to make investments during this period. Gambling should be halted temporarily.

The Fourth Month (6 May – 5 June)

Good wine needs no bush

Because of the appearance of several Lucky Stars within the Sign, Oxen will be pretty lucky in both business and money affairs this month. Their imagination and creativity will be highly inspired this month, so that they can handle their work more easily without too many problems. Most important of all, their outstanding performance will be highly appreciated by their superiors. Oxen will therefore be promoted sooner or later, but should keep in mind that they should try to be humble enough not to arouse any jealousy after their promotion. Otherwise, their continued success will be minimized. If possible, Oxen should try to look for other outlets in business for future development during this period of time.

Oxen should not talk too much about themselves in front of their friends and lovers. This will just spoil their image seriously.

The fortune in money affairs will be on the upswing for Oxen this month. If they want to buy property or valuables, this month would be the right time. And this will also be the right time for investing their money in new businesses.

The Fifth Month (6 June – 6 July)

Love makes the world go round

Oxen will have a wonderful time this month. They will have high spirits in their daily life. They will appreciate the small, wonderful things in daily life that they have ignored for a long time. Oxen will become quite romantic and enjoy singing and dancing. Their heart will become quite tender and full of love and care. Their affections will influence the other people around them.

Oxen will be able to handle their daily work easily, and they should not rely upon any other people to do it for them. At the very least, they should supervise all the details by themselves.

Their expenses will easily get out of control this month, so Oxen should try to keep to their budget. If Oxen wish to send flowers or letters to their lovers, they will receive a nice surprise in return.

The Sixth Month (7 July – 7 August)

Old habits die hard

This is one of the most unfavourable months of the year for Oxen. Many unexpected problems and disputes will arise suddenly. In addition, there may be some legal problems involved too. Oxen should try never to lose their temper. They must keep calm and handle the various situations with patience. Any irrational action will only complicate matters. Oxen should try to get rid of their old habits during this period. Some of their habits are outdated, and they should try to get rid of them and keep up with the new pace of things. It's necessary for Oxen to try their best to get rid of their old habits at this stage, or they will be left far behind, or even be eliminated sooner or later.

Oxen will become quite unpopular in various social gatherings. They should try to behave themselves and never talk about others in public. They should try to ignore gossip.

If possible, Oxen should try to take a break or vacation. They will be much relaxed and refreshed after that.

The Seventh Month (8 August – 7 September)

Haste makes waste

The bad luck of last month is just like a thunderstorm to Oxen, but it's all over this month. Oxen will have much better luck at work. However, they should take action, step by step, and try never to rush themselves. There will be a lot of work for Oxen to do this month, and they have to take care of all the details carefully, or they will mess up the whole thing.

Oxen have to drive and walk carefully this month to ensure their personal safety. Haste means danger or even death to them. Be patient, and remember it's better to be safe than sorry.

This month is not a good month for Oxen to make any important investments because they will lose a lot of money by doing so. It would be much better if they could wait for some other time in the months to come. In love affairs, Oxen should try not to make a hasty decision, or they will be very sorry about that in the near future.

The Eighth Month (8 September – 7 October)

Many a little effort makes a miracle

Oxen will have to work very hard this month, but they should not complain about it. The more they work, the more they get. All their efforts added together will make a big contribution towards their future success. Without their hard work during this period, they can hardly expect to see important career breakthroughs at the end of the year. Apart from this, Oxen should try to reach out a helping hand to those in need. Their deeds will be handsomely rewarded very soon.

Oxen should be gentle and kind to the children around them during this period. And it's a very good idea for them to spend more time with family members at weekends.

The fortune in money affairs for Oxen will be quite prosperous this month. And they will have a wonderful time with their lovers in the second half of the month.

The Ninth Month (8 October – 6 November)

No pain, no gain

The luck of Oxen drops a little bit this month. They have to struggle very hard for their business survival, or they will be eliminated. Oxen have to stand very firm for themselves and have no other people to rely on. They should keep this motto in mind: 'No pain, no gain.' This is the time for Oxen to think about their attitude towards their career. Unless they can build up a positive manner at work now, their successes in the months to come will be badly damaged. Apart from this, their partners will also play a very important role in their success. A suitable and co-operative partner will give Oxen a big helping hand during this period of time.

The health of Oxen won't be stable this month, so they should take good care of themselves. They may have an operation sometime this month. However, they will be fully recovered very soon.

What Oxen have to worry about is their safety in water. They must take special precautions when they go swimming, diving or fishing.

This month is not the right time for Oxen to purchase valuable items. They will lose money by doing so. Apart from this, they should not try their luck in high-risk investments or gambling.

The Tenth Month (7 November – 6 December)

Once bitten, twice shy

This will be the last unfavourable month of the year for Oxen. Once they can overcome the obstacles in front of them now, there will be no more difficulties in the next two months.

Oxen will face a lot of personal disputes at work during this period, and it's necessary for them to try their best to eliminate as much misunderstanding as they can. Oxen may be easily cheated by the people around them, and they should take the lesson and never make the same mistake again. They should keep alert to traps in the future.

Oxen may lose money by listening to their friends or partners regarding investments. They should have their own ideas about these instead of just listening to others. If possible, it's better for Oxen to seek the professional opinion of experts.

Oxen should try to give up their personal pride and show their true feelings to their lover, or their relationship will be diminished in the near future.

The Eleventh Month (7 December – 5 January)

The early bird catches the worm

The luck of Oxen will be at the peak of the year during this month. Several good chances will knock at their doors, one after another. Oxen should try to develop a keen perception to choose the most suitable one from them as their next main target.

There will be a lot of work for Oxen to do and they have to work overtime to finish all of it on time. Oxen should not forget the motto, 'The early bird catches the worm.' If they are fast enough in action, Oxen will have a very good chance of success. Otherwise, they will be easily beaten by their opponents.

Oxen will have some luck in gambling and lucky draws, and their investments will bring them handsome profits. However, they should take good care of their belongings to avoid pickpockets and robbery.

This month, Oxen will have a romantic relationship with their lover. But they should not indulge themselves too much in entertainment. There is a lot of work waiting for them to finish.

The Twelfth Month (6 January – 3 February)

If you pay peanuts, you get monkeys

Although the luck of Oxen will be going down a little bit this month, they will still be quite productive and successful in their career. Of course, they must work hard, but their efforts during this period won't be wasted. They will gain nothing if they just fool around. Oxen should think carefully about new development at this stage. Most important of all, Oxen must try to make a generous offer to attract more talent to work together with them. They will be very successful in their business by doing so. But the story will be quite different if they are reluctant to make a good offer.

Oxen should be sincere and honest to their friends, and especially to their lover. They will be isolated if they are just fooling around. They will have a nice surprise in return if they show their care by sending gifts and flowers.

Although their health is in pretty good shape, Oxen should watch their diet. Most import of all, they must keep away from drugs and alcohol.

Using Feng Shui to Improve Fortune: Directions, Colours, Numbers and Lucky Charm

The ancient Chinese used the traditional Horoscope to predict their fortune on a yearly basis – they used the art of Feng Shui to improve their luck.

It was their belief that the application of tactical Feng Shui would change their bad luck into good, and make their good luck improve even more.

This same method is still effective in today's modern world.

There are four main elements which I will use in tactical Feng Shui:

- Lucky Directions
- Lucky Colours
- Lucky Numbers
- Lucky Charm

Oxen will have a pretty productive and successful year in 2002, so they should try to make good use of every minute of the year to upgrade and strengthen themselves. Their creativity will bring forth splendid achievements to them if Oxen really try hard enough. There will be jealousy and suspicion from the people around them for their success, so Oxen should try to be aggressive at work, yet humble when handling their personal relationships. It's necessary for Oxen to watch out for business and money traps, or they will lose a lot of money as a consequence. They must be more conservative about their investments and should not go too far beyond their capabilities in money affairs to avoid a sudden collapse.

Fortunately, Oxen will be quite healthy throughout the year. However, they must watch their food to avoid food poisoning and infections. And they have to watch their personal safety with extreme care during outdoor activities.

This won't be a romantic year for Oxen, and they should take it easy. It's necessary for Oxen to try to reach a mutual understanding with their lover if they wish to keep delicate relationships alive.

I would suggest applying the following Feng Shui tactics to improve luck so that Oxen don't have to worry too much about their fate within the year.

Lucky Directions

The most favourable directions of the year for Oxen are **Southeast**, **West** and **Northeast.** Oxen should sleep or sit in these directions if they wish to improve their fortune.

To make this procedure very simple, divide the house or room into nine imaginary squares. Then, using a compass, check the exact direction of each square as shown in Figure 8. This will help to ensure that you do not make a mistake with the direction.

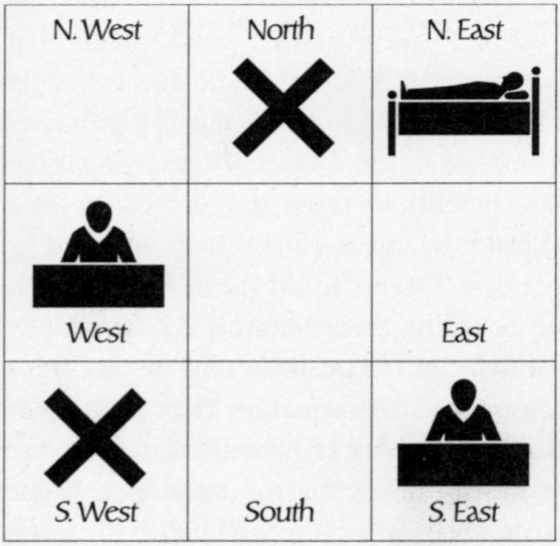

Figure 8

Oxen should sit in Southeast and West at work or while studying; this will ensure that their achievements are much greater than the Stars intended. To improve health and achieve a good night's sleep, Oxen should position the bed in the favourable direction shown (Northeast).

However, Oxen should try to keep away from the unfavourable directions of the year – that is, Southwest and North, as shown in Figure 8. Oxen should try not to sit, work or sleep in these directions, so as to get rid of the negative influences lurking there.

Lucky Colours

According to Chinese tradition, each of the five elements has its own representative colours. Fire is represented by red, pink and purple, Earth by yellow and brown, and so on. As a Feng Shui Master I would suggest **white, blue, grey** and **black** as Oxen's lucky colours for the year 2002.

Use these colours in paints, wall coverings, rugs, drapes and curtains. This will be sure to bring good fortune within the year.

However, Oxen should try not to use yellow or brown in 2002, to avoid bad luck.

Lucky Numbers

The lucky numbers for Oxen in 2002 are: **4** and **9**.

Fortune will be much improved by using these lucky numbers whenever possible. For example, if Oxen have a choice, the phone number 2494-4994 is better than 2534-1166 – because the former contains more fours and nines, Oxen's two lucky numbers for the year.

Lucky Charm

Feng Shui Masters believe that special objects can be used as a medium between human beings and nature. The fortune of the recipient is greatly improved as the positive wave of energy from nature is passed through the object or 'lucky charm' on to the recipient.

The lucky charm for the Oxen in 2002 is a stone statue of three toads playing with a pearl. A toad with a big coin in its mouth, in Chinese mythology, was considered to have the magic to bring fortune to human beings. Three toads together signifies various money sources. This statue has the meaning of 'abundant incomes from different sources'. For best results, it should be put in the west direction of the house.

Chapter Nine

The

Tiger

Years of the Tiger

1914 (4/Feb/14—4/Feb/15)   1962 (4/Feb/62—3/Feb/63)
1926 (4/Feb/26—4/Feb/27)   1974 (4/Feb/74—3/Feb/75)
1938 (4/Feb/38—4/Feb/39)   1986 (4/Feb/86—3/Feb/87)
1950 (4/Feb/50—3/Feb/51)   1998 (4/Feb/98—3/Feb/99)

If you have any doubt about the classification of the 12 animal signs, or the divisions of months and years, please refer to pages xiii–xiv.

Distribution of the Stars within the Sign for 2002

Lucky Stars	Unlucky Stars
None	Pointing at the Back
	Fierce Hercules
	Swallowed Up
	White Tiger
	Earthly Threat

Unlucky Stars
Pointing at the Back

Based on their long struggle for survival, the ancient Chinese realized that the most dangerous enemies were those behind one's back. Such people lay in wait for an opportunity to attack, either verbally or physically, without warning.

When this Star appears, people need to hide their weaknesses and be aware of any hidden enemies or gossip around them.

Fierce Hercules

Fei Lian is the name of a famous Chinese Hercules who served the wicked Emperor Zhou of the Shang Dynasty. His hot temper and tremendous energy brought considerable destruction to his people. To live in peace they tried to keep out of his way and not irritate him.

The appearance of this Star is a bad omen. People will be seriously hurt physically and financially if they provoke their superiors.

Swallowed Up

The ancient Chinese peasants faced numerous threats to their possessions. Their grain might be swallowed up by birds, their poultry and domestic animals might be swallowed up by wolves and tigers and, in their barns, their stored food might be swallowed up by rats or bandits.

When this Star appears, people have to take good care of their belongings and protect what they have worked hard to earn from other people.

White Tiger

In ancient China, it was the tiger, and not the lion, who was considered king of the jungle. The white tiger was the most fierce and feared of all tigers, and gradually became a symbol of violence and danger.

When this Star appears, people need to stay alert for danger and sudden attacks, which could turn them into helpless victims.

The ancient Chinese believed that malevolent spirits brought dangers and problems into their daily lives. Of these, 'Earthly Threat' was considered to be the least dangerous and damaging of the four 'Threats' in the Chinese Horoscope.

When this Star appears, people should be extra careful about road safety.

General Overview of the Year

This won't be a very good productive year for Tigers in business. Because of the appearance of several Unlucky Stars and the absence of a Lucky Star within their Sign, Tigers will have to struggle very hard for their survival in their careers. But struggle without good planning will gain Tigers nothing at work this year. Unless Tigers are able to come up with a good strategy for their business development, most of their efforts will be wasted.

The appearance of Unlucky Star 'Pointing at the Back' indicates that Tigers must try to keep their eyes wide open to watch out for hidden enemies, or they might be attacked from behind, which could be quite dangerous to them. Probably, Tigers will become the focus of gossip and criticism. Unless they can keep a low profile and keep silent, there will be endless trouble for them throughout the year.

Tigers should keep in mind that this won't be a good year for them to carry out important projects or to change jobs, because their chance of success would be quite slim.

This is definitely not a profitable year for Tigers, so they must try to watch their expenses and investments closely or they will lose a lot of money. The appearance of the Unlucky Star 'Swallowed Up' indicates that Tigers must try their best to take good care of their belongings and protect what they have worked hard to earn from other people. If possible, Tigers must try to pay all their bills as soon as possible, because any delay will be dangerous and costly.

Tigers will be in pretty good shape physically and mentally this year. The only thing that they have to worry about is their personal safety, especially their road safety. They should walk and drive with extreme care throughout the year.

Unfortunately, Tigers won't have too much luck in love affairs this year. But there's nothing much they can do about this. Under the circumstances, Tigers should keep in mind the motto, 'Easy does it.'

Career   *
Money   *
Health   * *
Love   *

* * = Fair/* = Unsatisfactory

Career *

Tigers won't have too much luck at work this year, and it will be necessary for them to put in extra time and effort to overcome the difficulties in their business. Their hard work plus a good strategy will help Tigers to survive under heavy pressure from a tight working schedule and strong challenges from opponents.

Tigers will be bothered very much by hidden enemies from time to time throughout the year, so it will be very important for them to hide their weaknesses to prevent their enemies from making use of them as weapons to attack them with. Tigers must handle their business with special care during the first, third, fourth, fifth, seventh, eighth and the last two months of the year. However, they will have better luck at work during the second, sixth and ninth months. They should try to make good use of these times if they wish to see better achievements in business during the year.

Money *

Unfortunately, this won't be a fortunate year in money affairs for Tigers. It's necessary for them to try to cut their extravagant habits and keep a tight budget to avoid financial problems. Apart from this, Tigers have to keep their eyes wide open to watch out for money traps, or they will lose a lot of cash. If Tigers are able to find the leaks in their financial systems on time, and try to do something about them, they will be in a much better situation.

Tigers must pay special attention to taking care of their money affairs during the first, third, fourth, fifth, eighth and the last two months of the year.

Health **

Tigers will not have too much to worry about their health this year, because they will be in a pretty good condition physically and mentally. But, because of the appearance of the Unlucky Star 'Earthly Threat', Tigers must mind their personal safety, especially their road safety. They must drive with extreme care during the last two months of the year. Apart from this, they must watch their safety on trips during the third and seventh months. Most important of all, Tigers should try not to stay on the streets too late at night to avoid street violence during the tenth month.

Love *

Tigers will be deeply disappointed if they are longing for a passionate romance this year. Although they might have tried their best to impress their lover, all their efforts will be in vain. However, Tigers will have better luck in love affairs during the second, sixth, ninth and eleventh months of the year. 'Faith will move mountains' – Tigers should keep this in mind, and there may be miracles for them in love affairs during these four months. Their relationship with their lover might be threatened during the fourth, seventh, eighth and the last month. Unless they can try their best to do something about this, Tigers will have to face a broken relationship with their lover.

Monthly In-depth Forecasts
The First Month (4 February – 5 March)

The walls have ears

This will not be a good year for Tigers, and they will have a pretty sluggish start to the beginning of the year. Besides numerous difficulties at work, Tigers will have numerous personal disputes too. In this situation, Tigers should try to concentrate on their business only and forget about gossip and disputes for the time being. Tigers have to keep in mind that they must not talk about others, especially their superiors, or their career will be seriously jeopardized. During this month there will be no secrets in their office, because the walls have ears.

This won't be a profitable month for Tigers. Therefore, they should forget about trying their luck in investments and gambling. There will probably be some unexpected expenses at the end of the month.

Tigers should try to be loyal and honest to their lover, because cheats never prosper. They will feel quite lonely during this period, but there's nothing they can do about it at this stage.

The Second Month (6 March – 4 April)

Easy does it

The fortune of Tigers improves a lot this month. They should try to pick up some momentum at work during this period, or they will be left far behind. However, Tigers should not be too ambitious, or they will be isolated or repelled. In other words, Tigers should not try to push people around in order to fulfil their ambitions. Co-operation will be much better than cruel competition. It's important for Tigers to improve their relationship with colleagues and clients; this will assure much better business development in the months to come.

Tigers will have a pretty romantic period this month. Probably, they will have the chance to meet someone very attractive at the beginning of the month, but they should not be too aggressive. Easy does it.

This will be a profitable month for Tigers. Their income will be much improved. Apart from this, they will have luck in lottery and lucky draws near the end of the month.

The Third Month (5 April – 5 May)

When in doubt, do nowt

Tigers will face certain drastic changes at work this month, and they will be quite confused what with all the new and unfamiliar situations. Tigers will be easily defeated if they lose their patience and confidence under the pressure. It's necessary for them to keep calm and try not to make any hasty decisions. Strictly speaking, Tigers should not do too much for the time being if they are not quite sure about their future. If necessary, Tigers would be better off asking for professional advice from experts before they make up their mind.

The fortune in money affairs for Tigers will fluctuate this month, so it would not be wise for them to make investments during this period. Apart from this, Tigers must try not to borrow money within the month, or they will be in big trouble.

Tigers must watch their personal safety when they go out on trips. In addition, they should watch their wallets and passports too.

The Fourth Month (6 May – 5 June)

Don't put all your eggs in one basket

This will be one of the most unfavourable months of the year for Tigers. Their major concern during this period is how to save themselves from financial difficulties. They should try to diversify their investments, and not to put all their eggs in one basket. It would not be wise for them to buy property or valuables, or they will be very sorry about that soon. Tigers must try to pay their bills as soon as possible.

Tigers should try their best to handle their business by themselves, because they will have no one to depend on. They have to stand up firmly for themselves. This is definitely not a suitable time for Tigers to carry out new projects, or they will meet with numerous challenges and objections.

There will be quarrels and fights between Tigers and their lover during this month. They should try to calm themselves down, and try to settle their conflicts with patience as soon as possible.

The Fifth Month (6 June – 6 July)

Lend your money and lose your friend

Although the luck of Tigers will improve a little bit, there will be several problems left over for them to solve during the first half of the month. Money affairs will bother them again this month. Tigers have to try to cut their extravagant tastes and habits, or they will face financial problems. Tigers may be asked to lend their money; they'd better reject this kind of request, or they will not only lose their money, but also lose their friends.

This is definitely not a good time for Tigers to risk their money in gambling.

Tigers should not start any new projects or change jobs within this month. They should wait for some other suitable time.

Because the time is just not right, Tigers should try not to be too ambitious during this period. Instead, they should try to concentrate on their present job without too many distractions.

Tigers will suffer from different kinds of infection during this period. Therefore, they should take as much rest as they can, and stay away from crowded places. Apart from this, they had better watch food and drink carefully to avoid food poisoning.

The Sixth Month (7 July – 7 August)

A mouse may help a lion

This will be one of the most favourable months of the year for Tigers. The heavy workload of last month will be much relieved now, and Tigers will be able to handle their daily work with ease during this period. In addition, Tigers may have some unexpected support from their subordinates, or from some quarter they would not have anticipated. Tigers should not be too proud to turn down the offer of help, or they will miss a very good chance. Don't forget the motto, 'A mouse may help a lion.' This will come true during this period. Tigers should try to be more practical and stop fooling around this month if they want to be more successful in the months to come.

The fortune of Tigers in money affairs will be quite good this month. If they want to get more income from different sources, they will be quite successful during this period. However, they should try to save more money now for the rainy days to come at the end of the year.

With the help of their friends, Tigers will have a very good chance to meet their dream-lover. Unfortunately, it won't be easy for them to hold on to this delicate relationship.

The Seventh Month (8 August – 7 September)

It never rains but it pours

There is a sudden thunderstorm for Tigers this month. They will face a lot of difficulties in different aspects during this period of time. Unless they are well prepared beforehand, Tigers will be totally confused. Their contracts may be denied, agreements may be broken, requests may be turned down, applications may be rejected – all these kinds of misfortune will appear one after another this month. Not too many people can survive under these circumstances if they don't equip themselves psychologically beforehand. Tigers should stand firmly so that they aren't washed away for ever with the storm.

If possible, Tigers should try to take a break or vacation this month. However, they should pay more attention to their health and safety when travelling. They must curb their curiosity and try to stay away from dangerous places. Apart from this, they should try to keep away from wild animals too.

Unless Tigers have tried their best to show their tenderness to their lover, they will face a broken relationship. In addition, Tigers may be somewhat isolated by their friends and relatives during this period.

The Eighth Month (8 September – 7 October)

Self-preservation is the first law of nature

Tigers won't be released too much from the heavy pressure at work just yet. They still have to face a lot of problems in many areas. They will meet several strong challenges in and out of the office, so they should try to protect themselves from being eliminated. It's necessary for them to know how to protect themselves from becoming the target of criticism and spite. Tigers must try their best to hide their weaknesses and true feelings during this critical moment.

Telling white lies to their friends and lover may be helpful for the time being if Tigers are to maintain a good relationship with them. If they have to face a broken relationship during the month, Tigers should try to accept this. Any radical and irrational behaviour will only bring about a terrible end.

This is definitely not a profitable month for Tigers. They should try to keep their eyes wide open to business and money traps, or they will lose a lot of cash. Apart from this, they must keep their windows and doors safely locked to avoid a burglary or break-in in the middle of the month.

The Ninth Month (8 October – 6 November)

Laugh and the world laughs with you

Almost all of the troubles brought on by the 'storms' of the last two months will be gone this period. Tigers will be much refreshed and will be able to regain much of their energy and confidence this month. This will be the suitable time for them to work hard to catch up on the pace at work if they don't want to be left too far behind. However, Tigers should try to keep themselves in high spirits. Just as the motto says, 'Laugh and the world laughs with you.' Their high spirits will help them very much at work. They must not turn a cold shoulder to partners or subordinates.

There may be a second chance for Tigers in their love affairs. However, if they fail to achieve mutual understanding with their lover, this romance won't last long.

Tigers will be busily engaged in social affairs this month. They will be quite popular among their new acquaintances, but they should mind their tongue to avoid unnecessary trouble.

The Tenth Month (7 November – 6 December)

Let sleeping dogs lie

Tigers should try not to provoke their superiors this month, or their career will be seriously damaged. Even verbal protests or criticism about their superiors will create problems for Tigers. In other words, Tigers should try to keep a safe distance from their superiors if they want to keep their job. Apart from this, if Tigers are wise enough, they should try to avoid attracting the attention of competitors. Keeping a low profile will save them a lot of trouble. In the mean time, Tigers should try to strengthen themselves by reading and learning more in order to build a more solid foundation for their future development.

Tigers will be quite weak physically this month, so they should take good care of themselves. They have to put on more clothes to avoid a bad cold. In addition, they should not stay out in the streets too late at night, or they may become the victim of street violence near the end of the month.

Although their fortune in money affairs won't be too bad this month, Tigers should be more conservative in handling their money. They have nothing to worry about so long as they are not too greedy.

The Eleventh Month (7 December – 5 January)

If you run after two hares, you will catch neither

The last two months won't be a good period of time for Tigers. They have to fight very hard for their survival in business. There will be different kinds of challenges from different sources, and Tigers should try to face them with extreme care. It would not be wise to fight against two enemies at the same time, so Tigers should try not to commit this mistake or they will be badly defeated.

Apart from this, Tigers should try to concentrate on one project only and not to diversify in too many different areas during this period of time. Just as the motto says, 'If you run after two hares, you will catch neither.' Tigers will end up with nothing if they lose their concentration.

Although there might be several attractive others on offer, Tigers should not try to fool around with them, or they may face an unexpected sad ending.

This is definitely not a profitable month for Tigers. They should not risk their money in investments or gambling.

At the end of the month, Tigers should watch out carefully for the danger of fire at home.

The Twelfth Month (6 January – 3 February)

What can't be cured must be endured

Tigers will face a very difficult period of time at year end. Fortunately, they will have much better luck next year. But first of all, they have to face reality and try to solve their present problems. One thing they have to keep in mind is that, no matter how difficult things might be, Tigers must take them calmly. Just like the motto says, 'What can't be cured must be endured.' Tigers should take their defeats as lessons and try not to make the same mistakes in future. What they cannot afford to lose at the moment is their confidence. They will have a second chance to start all over again sooner or later if they can keep their confidence.

This won't have been a romantic year for Tigers, and they may have been hurt several times in love affairs. However, they should keep themselves in high spirits and try their best not to bury themselves in sorrow. Their romantic life will turn over a new leaf at the end of the year.

Again, this will not be a profitable month for Tigers, so they should try to save more money for unexpected expenses towards the end of the year. Try to keep alert to avoid being cheated in gambling.

Using Feng Shui to Improve Fortune:
Directions, Colours, Numbers and Lucky Charm

The ancient Chinese used the traditional Horoscope to predict their fortune on a yearly basis – they used the art of Feng Shui to improve their luck.

It was their belief that the application of tactical Feng Shui would change their bad luck into good, and make their good luck improve even more.

This same method is still effective in today's modern world.

There are four main elements which I will use in tactical Feng Shui:

◆ Lucky Directions
◆ Lucky Colours
◆ Lucky Numbers
◆ Lucky Charm

Tigers will have to struggle very hard for their survival in business during 2002. A good strategy plus their diligence will help Tigers to get out from difficulties, otherwise they will become the sure loser at year end. Most important of all, Tigers must try to discover their hidden enemies and prevent attacks from behind, because these could prove quite dangerous. Tigers should try not to make drastic changes at work or to carry out new projects, because their chances of success will be quite slim during the year.

This is definitely not a profitable year for Tigers, so they must try to watch their expenses and investments carefully, or they will lose a lot of money. Fortunately, Tigers will be in pretty good shape physically and mentally. Therefore, they don't have too much to worry about on this score, apart from their road safety. They must walk and drive with extreme care throughout the year. Tigers won't have too much luck in love affairs. They should not be frustrated too much by this, or both their private and business life will be totally messed up.

I would suggest applying the following Feng Shui tactics to improve luck so that Tigers don't have to worry too much about their fate within the year.

Lucky Directions

The most favourable directions of the year for Tigers are **West**, **Northwest** and **Northeast**. Tigers should sleep or sit in these directions if they wish to improve their fortune.

To make this procedure very simple, divide the house or room into nine imaginary squares. Then, using a compass, check the exact direction of each square as shown in Figure 9. This will help to ensure that you do not make a mistake with the direction.

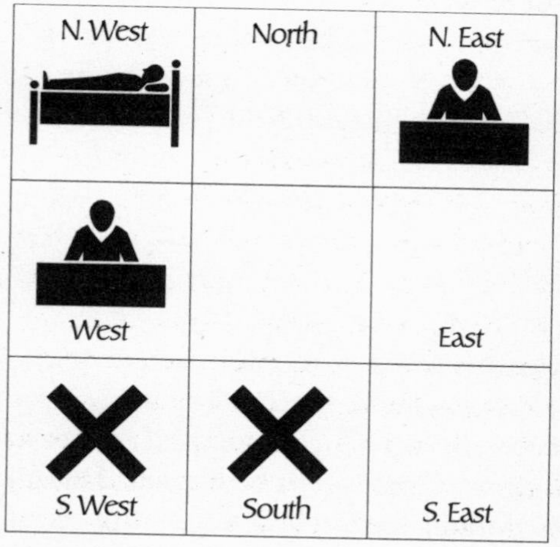

N. West	North	N. East
West		East
S. West	South	S. East

Figure 9

Tigers should sit in West and Northeast at work or while studying; this will ensure that their achievements are much greater than the Stars intended. To improve health and achieve a good night's sleep, Tigers should position the bed in the favourable direction shown (Northwest).

However, Tigers should try to keep away from the unfavourable directions of the year – that is, South and Southwest, as shown in Figure 9. Tigers should try not to sit, work or sleep in these directions, so as to get rid of the negative influences lurking there.

Lucky Colours

According to Chinese tradition, each of the five elements has its own representative colours. Fire is represented by red, pink and purple, Earth by yellow and brown, and so on. As a Feng Shui Master I would suggest **red**, **purple** and **green** as Tiger's lucky colours for the year 2002.

Use these colours in paints, wall coverings, rugs, drapes and curtains. This will be sure to bring good fortune within the year.

However, Tigers should try not to use white or black in 2002, to avoid bad luck.

Lucky Numbers

The lucky numbers for Tigers in 2002 are: **2** and **8**.

Fortune will be much improved by using these lucky numbers whenever possible. For example, if Tigers have a choice, the phone number 2287-8228 is better than 2368-1122 – because the former contains more twos and eights, Tiger's two lucky numbers for the year.

Lucky Charm

Feng Shui Masters believe that special objects can be used as a medium between human beings and nature. The fortune of the recipient is greatly improved as the positive wave of energy from nature is passed through the object or 'lucky charm' on to the recipient.

The lucky charm for the Tiger is a rabbit and a sheep, both resting their front legs on stones. A branch of plum and Chinese character 'happiness' are inscribed on the stones separately. A rabbit with plum and a sheep with 'happiness' have the same pronunciation in Chinese has 'to become very successful and well admired'. For best results, this lucky charm should be put in the northeast direction of the house.

Chapter Ten

The
Rabbit

Years of the Rabbit

1915 (5/Feb/15—4/Feb/16)   1963 (4/Feb/63—4/Feb/64)
1927 (5/Feb/27—4/Feb/28)   1975 (4/Feb/75—4/Feb/76)
1939 (5/Feb/39—4/Feb/40)   1987 (4/Feb/87—3/Feb/88)
1951 (4/Feb/51—4/Feb/52)   1999 (4/Feb/99—3/Feb/00)

If you have any doubt about the classification of the 12 animal signs, or the divisions of months and years, please refer to pages xiii–xiv.

Distribution of the Stars within the Sign for 2002

Lucky Stars	Unlucky Stars
Heavenly Virtue	Pool of Indulgence
Blessing Virtue	Tongues Wag
Star of Blessing	Funeral Robe
Heavenly Happiness	

Lucky Stars
Heavenly Virtue

Virtue was highly appreciated by Confucius, the great Chinese philosopher. The ancient Chinese believed that virtue not only set a good example to others, but provided its own benefits and rewards as well. The Chinese Horoscope has four 'Virtue' Stars, with Heavenly Virtue being the most influential.

The appearance of this Star is definitely a very good omen. It minimizes negative influences from the Unlucky Stars, and bestows a peaceful and joyful year.

Blessing Virtue

This is another 'Virtue' Star in the Chinese Horoscope. When this Star appears, people will enjoy a year full of blessings from other people. Its message is that it is best to set a good example and be kind to those who have been helpful in the past. By following the practice of 'one good turn deserves another', blessings will manifest continually.

Star of Blessing

During Chinese New Year it is customary to decorate the home with a prominent piece of red paper on which the Chinese character 'Blessing' is printed, in hopes of bringing good luck. Similarly, in the Chinese Horoscope the presence of the 'Star of Blessing' is considered to be most lucky.

This Star indicates a very fortunate year. It can even change bad luck to good.

Heavenly Happiness

The Chinese have always considered marriage to be one of the greatest blessings in life. It not only brings the joys of family life, but also helps to perpetuate the family, hopefully for generations to come. Such a gift is considered to be heaven-sent. This Star symbolizes marital happiness and is highly regarded in the Chinese Horoscope.

The presence of this Star signifies romance, a healing of broken relationships, and possibly even marriage before the year is out.

Unlucky Stars
Pool of Indulgence

One of China's most cruel and wicked emperors, Emperor Zhou of the Shang Dynasty, built a pool which he filled with wine inside his luxurious palace. He invited his royal followers and beautiful women to come and be merry by drinking or even swimming in the wine. This symbol of over-indulgence warns against bad habits and self-indulgent behaviour.

If this Star appears within the Sign, people need to avoid bad habits – if they don't, they will miss out on good opportunities and waste a great deal of money.

Tongues Wag

Confucianism endorses the adage 'Silence is Golden.' In ancient Chinese society, gossiping – especially rumour-mongering – was definitely looked down upon.

Should this Star appear within a Sign it is a warning to people to refrain from gossip. Wagging tongues will not only hurt others, but the person who spreads gossip as well.

Funeral Robe

During traditional Chinese funerals, people would wear roughly-tailored yellow hemp clothes as a symbol of their grief, showing they were too overwhelmed with sorrow to worry about finery. Since then these yellow robes have come to symbolize funerals.

The appearance of this Star is not a good omen. It signifies that people need to be alert to potential medical problems among older family members – periodic medical check-ups and, if necessary, effective treatment should be undertaken regularly.

General Overview of the Year

This will be a very productive and prosperous year for Rabbits because of the appearances of several Lucky Stars within their Sign. If they would like to carry out important new projects, this year would be a very suitable time to do so. There will be several opportunities knocking at their doors from time to time throughout the year; it's up to Rabbits to seize them or not. If they are too hesitant in taking action, these opportunities will slip through their fingers and will never come back again. They'd have no one to blame but themselves for that.

Even though Rabbits may encounter some difficulties from time to time, they will be able to overcome them without too many difficulties. Rabbits will become quite creative and innovative at work this year, so they will have splendid achievements in business by year's end. But they have to remind themselves that they should never let their private affairs get mixed up with business, or they will spoil everything. 'Business before pleasure' should be their motto at work during the year.

This will be a fortunate year for Rabbits. They will have a pretty good income from different sources, but they have to watch their expenses very carefully. Otherwise, Rabbits would probably spend much more money on entertainment than they might ever have anticipated, and this could bring about terrible financial consequences.

Rabbits won't have too much to worry about regarding their health this year. However, they must try not to over-indulge in sex and alcohol, or their health will be seriously hurt both physically and mentally.

This will be a very romantic year for Rabbits. But the appearance of the Unlucky Star 'Pool of Indulgence' indicates that Rabbits might tend to indulge themselves in sex and alcohol too much. It's necessary for them to cut that out as much as they can. However, Rabbits will have a very good chance to get married within the year, mainly due to the appearance of the Lucky Star 'Heavenly Happiness' within their Sign.

Career	* * * *
Money	* * *
Health	* *
Love	* * * *

* * * * = Very Fortunate/* * * = Pretty Good/* * = Fair

Career * * * *

Rabbits will be quite productive at work this year because of the appearance of several Lucky Stars within their Sign. They will be full of energy and creativity in business, and they should try to make use of this period of time to carry out their important projects.

Opportunities will keep knocking on their doors one after another throughout the year. Tigers should not hesitate too much in taking action to seize these, or they will have no one to blame but themselves. 'Business before pleasure' should be their motto. Rabbits will be able to reach splendid achievements at work during the first, second, fourth, seventh, tenth and the last month of the year. However, they should try to pay special attention to their business to avoid problems during the third, fifth, sixth, eighth and ninth months.

Money * * *

Rabbits will be quite fortunate in money affairs this year. They will have plenty of income from different sources, and their luck in lotteries and gambling will be quite good occasionally. The only thing that they should worry about is their extravagance. Probably, they will spend much more money on entertainment than they'd ever anticipated. Their indulgence in sex and alcohol will not only spoil their health, but their finances too. Rabbits should try to take particular care of their money affairs during the third, fifth, sixth, eighth and eleventh months. However, they will have much better luck in investments and gambling during the first, second, seventh, tenth and the last month of the year.

Health **

Rabbits will be quite healthy this year and they will have nothing to worry about except for their tendency to over-indulge in sex and alcohol. Unless they can do something about this, their health will be seriously hurt physically and mentally. Because of the appearance of the Unlucky Star 'Funeral Robe' within their Sign, Rabbits must take good care of elderly family members during the year. If anything goes wrong with them, Rabbits must take them to the doctor or hospital for immediate medical treatment. Rabbits should mind themselves during the third, seventh and ninth months of the year.

Love ****

This will be a very romantic year for Rabbits. They will be quite popular. However they should not indulge themselves too much in sex and entertainments, or both their health and business will be spoiled. One thing they should keep in mind is that they should never let their personal affairs get mixed up with their business affairs. If Rabbits don't mess about with several lovers at the same time, they will have a very good chance to get married within the year. Rabbits have to take good care of their love affairs during the second, fifth, sixth, eighth and tenth months.

Monthly In-depth Forecasts
The First Month (4 February – 5 March)

Diligence is the mother of good luck

This will be a pretty fortunate year for Rabbits. Their popularity among colleagues and clients will help them to achieve good things in business. They will have a very good start to the year, and they had better try to make good use of it, or they are going to miss a very good opportunity at work. The more they work, the more good will be their harvest this month. 'Diligence is the mother of good luck.' Rabbits should keep this motto in mind. As a matter of fact, this month will be the best time for Rabbits to carry out new projects or change jobs, because they will meet with fewer obstacles at the beginning stage.

Rabbits will be busily engaged in different social gatherings, and they will be quite popular. However, they should try not to indulge themselves too much in love affairs, or they will be in big trouble in the very near future.

The fortune of Rabbits in money affairs will be quite good this month. They will be able to receive a good return from their investments during this period. Apart from this, they will have luck in gambling and lucky draws too.

The Second Month (6 March – 4 April)

A gossip carries talk both ways

Although the fortune of Rabbits will drop down a little bit this month, they will have a pretty productive month at work. They should try to work hard enough to earn more credit for themselves in their career. They should try not to fool around during this period, because they will fool nobody but themselves by doing so.

However, their major concern of the month is communication. As the 'Tongues Wag' Unlucky Star appears within their Sign, so Rabbits will be easily involved in gossip. Unless they can keep silent and keep away from gossip, Rabbits will be hurt deeply in both their business and private life. The best thing for them to do is to try to keep secrets in their heart and never speak out to anybody during this period.

There will be some rumours about Rabbits in love affairs. They should not get angry about this. Instead, they should try to explain themselves to their lover with patience and sincerity. One thing they should never do this month is to cheat their lover, or they will surely be very sorry about that.

Fortunately, Rabbits will have good luck both in investments and gambling. But they should not be too greedy, because their fortune will fluctuate near month's end.

The Third Month (5 April – 5 May)

Fairly and softly go far in a day

Rabbits should try not to be too ambitious or aggressive in their business or private life. They will lose popularity with colleagues and friends as a result, and that will hurt them seriously during this period of time. What they should do is try to co-operate rather than fight. Rabbits must try to solve conflicts with a fair and soft approach; this will be the most effective way to success in business and in their private life this month. Forgiveness will be a very good remedy for Rabbits in solving their personal problems and disputes.

The major concern for Rabbits during this month is their personal safety. They must walk with extreme care in the middle of the month. Don't rush, it's better late than never. Apart from this, Rabbits should not risk their life when they go swimming or diving.

The fortune of Rabbits will be sluggish during this period. It would not be wise for them to risk their money in investments or gambling. They should be more conservative in handling their money affairs.

The Fourth Month (6 May – 5 June)

The better the day, the better the deed

Chances will keep knocking at the door this month. Rabbits will be quite successful this month, but they must try to be humble enough to avoid jealousy. There will be endless trouble following after them if they become too proud after their success at work. If they are clever enough, Rabbits should give credit to those who work with them. They will have even greater successes in the months to come by doing so. In other words, if they foster good morale by setting a good example, Rabbits will be able to become the masters of their good fortune throughout the year.

Rabbits will be in good health this month. However, they should take good care of elderly family members. If anything goes wrong with them, Rabbits should take them to see a doctor to have proper treatment as soon as possible.

Although the fortune of Rabbits will be much improved this month, they should try to keep to a tight budget. Otherwise, they are sure to have financial problems in the following five months. It's better to save for the coming rainy days at this stage.

The Fifth Month (6 June – 6 July)

Cheats never prosper

Bad luck will come as suddenly as a thunderstorm this month, so Rabbits should try to be more cautious in handling their business or they will suffer a bitter and unexpected defeat. Different kinds of problems will come up one after the other in both their business and private life, and Rabbits must handle them patiently and calmly. Fortunately, their bad luck will go swiftly, like a thunderstorm, at the end of the month. In any case, Rabbits should try not to start any new projects or to make any important changes in their career.

The major concern for Rabbits during this period of time is to try to be honest to clients, co-workers and friends. They must not play tricks this month, because cheats never prosper. They will be in big legal trouble if they try to break the law.

Rabbits will face severe tests in their love affairs this month. It's very important for them to build up mutual trust with their lover, or they may face a broken relationship very soon. Rabbits should never cheat their lover during this period.

Rabbits must keep their eyes wide open to make sure that they won't fall into money or business traps. If possible, Rabbits should try to keep away from wicked so-called friends. Drugs will lead them to total destruction and nowhere else.

The Sixth Month (7 July – 7 August)

Of two evils, choose the lesser

Rabbits will have to make several difficult decisions at work this month. If possible, they should ask advice from experts to help them to make the proper choice. They would put themselves in a very difficult situation if they failed to do so. The situation will become even worse if they hesitate to make up their mind and let things go out of control. Making the right decision without too much delay is the key to their survival during this period.

Probably, Rabbits will have to make a difficult decision in their love affairs too. How to choose between business and love, or how to make a choice between two lovers, will become a dilemma for Rabbits during this month. If they try to bury their heads in the sand, Rabbits will be in big trouble in the months to come.

This won't be a profitable month for Rabbits. They will spend much more money on entertainments than they ever anticipated, so they should try their best to watch their expenses.

The Seventh Month (8 August – 7 September)

Eagles don't catch flies

This will be one of the most favourable months of the year for Rabbits. They will have important breakthroughs at work during this period if they work hard enough. If they approach their clients or superiors properly and promptly, Rabbits will be able to be a sure winner in business. However, Rabbits should try not to diversify too much at work, or their energy and time will be somewhat wasted. In other words, Rabbits should try to concentrate on important targets only, or their chances of success will be much damaged. If the eagle chases after flies, it ends up with nothing big in hand. Rabbits should take lesson to mind.

Rabbits should try not to indulge too much in sex and alcohol this month, or their health will be badly hurt. Most important of all, they should try not to fool around with several lovers at the same time during this period.

This will be a profitable month for Rabbits. Although their income will increase during this period, they should try not to risk their money in gambling. Apart from this, they have to watch out for pickpockets near the end of the month.

The Eighth Month (8 September – 7 October)

Empty vessels make the most sound

This month and next month will be the most unfavourable for Rabbits. They have to be more cautious in handling their business, and try to be more conservative if they don't want to have a sudden big fall. Rabbits will become helpless victims in front of their competitors if they don't know how to hide their weaknesses at work. Rabbits must keep their mouth shut when they face unfamiliar matters. Their silence will hide their ignorance, and uphold their image. It's better for Rabbits to keep away from talkative people for the time being, or there will be endless trouble following after them. They should keep in mind that 'Out of gossip, out of trouble.'

This is definitely not a profitable month for Rabbits. They should not make any investments during this period, or they will lose much more money than they'd ever anticipated. Apart from this, Rabbits should take good care of their accounts, and try not to let other people fool them in this matter. Rabbits must try to keep their financial situation top secret, and try not to let anyone know about it.

Rabbits must know what to say and when to talk to their lover this month, or there will be numerous quarrels. In other words, the more they talk, the more trouble they will have in love affairs.

The Ninth Month (8 October – 6 November)

You never miss the water till the well runs dry

Rabbits will have a very heavy workload this month, and they will be exhausted by it. However, they will be in a better situation if they know how to make good arrangements for themselves at work. A bad schedule will mess up the whole thing and bring terrible results to Rabbits. Apart from this, Rabbits must be friendly to their colleagues and clients, because they need their support at this critical moment. Without their help, Rabbits will be easily defeated.

This month, Rabbits should take good care of their health. They must try to get enough rest and sleep. One thing they must keep in mind is that they should not exhaust themselves by burning the candle at both ends. There will be year-long health problems waiting for them if they don't know how to take care of themselves.

Rabbits should cut out all their extravagant tastes and habits in order to save enough money for themselves. They won't know the bitterness of poverty until they run out of money.

The Tenth Month (7 November – 6 December)

Experience is the best teacher

The thunderstorm of the last two months will be all over during this period. Rabbits will have much better luck at work this month, so they should try to make good use of it. However, Rabbits should try not to rush, or they will tumble over obstacles in their haste at the beginning of the month. A good plan will help them a lot in their career. Rabbits should try to learn from experience in making plans for their future development. If Rabbits can't learn from their past experiences, and commit the same mistakes again, they will be badly defeated again in the near future.

The fortune of Rabbits in money affairs will be much improved this month. Now they can think about investing in new projects. Apart from this, they will have luck in gambling. But Rabbits have to take care of their wallets and other personal belongings when they go out at night.

Rabbits should show their care and tenderness to their lover in person during this period. They will get a nice surprise if they do so. Rabbits must try to be punctual for all appointments with lovers or close friends.

The Eleventh Month (7 December – 5 January)

All that glitters is not gold

Rabbits must try to keep their eyes wide open to watch out for pretenders. If they fail to do so, Rabbits will learn a costly lesson. They should keep in mind that they must not judge people according to their appearance. They should keep this motto in mind: 'All that glitters is not gold.' It would hurt Rabbits very much in their career if they were to choose the wrong partner. It's very important for them to find some capable and practical partners for their future business development. Rabbits must try to keep their business secret, or their chances of success will be much diminished.

In money affairs, Rabbits have to be more cautious in investments or they will be cheated. Some projects may seem to be quite attractive, but Rabbits will lose money in them eventually. Rabbits should wait for another time to make investments.

This will be a romantic month for Rabbits because they will be quite popular. However, they should try not to indulge themselves too much in sex, or their career will be somewhat damaged.

The Twelfth Month (6 January – 3 February)

Fortune favours the brave

Rabbits will gain important achievements if they have the guts to start new projects this month. They will miss a lot of chances if they are too hesitant in taking action. Once they have started their projects, everything will be fine and settled for them. Don't forget that time and tide wait for no man. It will be very difficult for Rabbits to find the same good chances later on if they pass them up now. Confidence and determination will be the most effective weapons for Rabbits to fight against difficulties in their career. They must have the guts to take challenges and defend their own rights during this period, or their chances and profits might be taken away by other people.

Rabbits will be quite healthy this month, but they should take care of the health and safety of elderly family members. If possible, Rabbits should spend more time with family members during this period of time.

This will be one of the most fortunate months of the year for Rabbits. Their investments will bring good profits to them sooner or later, and they will have luck in gambling and lucky draws too. This month will be a profitable time for them to buy property and valuables.

Using Feng Shui to Improve Fortune: Directions, Colours, Numbers and Lucky Charm

The ancient Chinese used the traditional Horoscope to predict their fortune on a yearly basis – they used the art of Feng Shui to improve their luck.

It was their belief that the application of tactical Feng Shui would change their bad luck into good, and make their good luck improve even more.

This same method is still effective in today's modern world.

There are four main elements which I will use in tactical Feng Shui:

◆ Lucky Directions
◆ Lucky Colours
◆ Lucky Numbers
◆ Lucky Charm

Rabbits will have a very prosperous and productive year in 2002. There will be opportunities knocking at their doors from time to time throughout the year, and Rabbits must try not to let them slip through their fingers. Rabbits will be quite creative and innovative at work, so they could have splendid achievements at year's end. However, Rabbits should never let their business and private life get mixed up with each other, or their chances of success will be seriously spoiled. 'Business before pleasure' should be their motto during the year.

Rabbits will be quite fortunate in money affairs. They will earn a pretty good income from different sources. However, their major concern this year is not how to earn more, but how to save more. Otherwise their money will be easy come, easy go.

If Rabbits don't indulge themselves in sex and alcohol, they will be in pretty good shape physically and mentally. Fortunately, this will be a very romantic year for Rabbits. They will have a very good chance of finding true love or getting married.

I would suggest applying the following Feng Shui tactics to ensure greater success throughout the year.

Lucky Directions

The most favourable directions of the year for Rabbits are **Southeast, Southwest** and **Northwest**. Rabbits should sleep or sit in these directions if they wish to improve their fortune.

To make this procedure very simple, divide the house or room into nine imaginary squares. Then, using a compass, check the exact direction of each square as shown in Figure 10. This will help to ensure that you do not make a mistake with the direction.

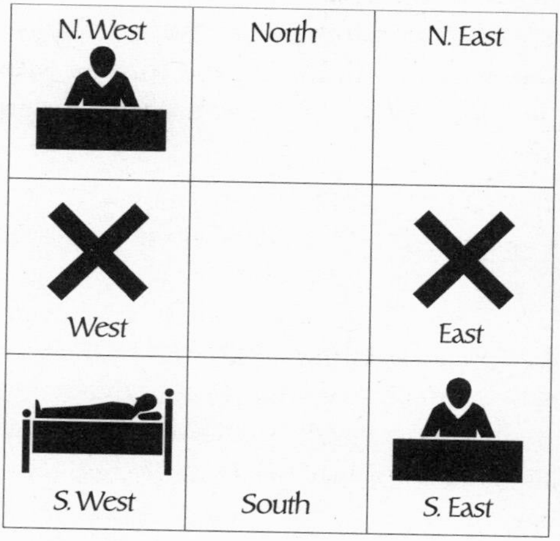

Figure 10

Rabbits should sit in Southeast or Northwest at work or while studying; this will ensure that their achievements are much greater than the Stars intended. To improve health and achieve a good night's sleep, Rabbits should position the bed in the favourable direction shown (Southwest).

However, Rabbits should try to keep away from the unfavourable directions of the year – that is, East and West, as shown in Figure 10. Rabbits should try not to sit, work or sleep in these directions, so as to get rid of the negative influences lurking there.

Lucky Colours

According to Chinese tradition, each of the five elements has its own representative colours. Fire is represented by red, pink and purple, Earth by yellow and brown, and so on. As a Feng Shui Master I would suggest **yellow**, **brown**, **red** and **orange** as Rabbit's lucky colours for the year 2002.

Use these colours in paints, wall coverings, rugs, drapes and curtains. This will be sure to bring good fortune within the year.

However, Rabbits should try not to use white or green in 2002, to avoid bad luck.

Lucky Numbers

The lucky numbers for Rabbits in 2002 are: 1 and 5.

Fortune will be much improved by using these lucky numbers whenever possible. For example, if Rabbits have a choice, the phone number 2112-5115 is better than 2682-4646 – because the former contains more ones and fives, Rabbit's two lucky numbers for the year.

Lucky Charm

Feng Shui Masters believe that special objects can be used as a medium between human beings and nature. The fortune of the recipient is greatly improved as the positive wave of energy from nature is passed through the object or 'lucky charm' on to the recipient.

The lucky charm for the Rabbit in 2002 is two pairs of rabbits with ganoderma in their mouths. In Chinese mythology, ganoderma was believed to have magical power and therefore eventually became the symbol of health longevity. For best results, this lucky charm should be put in the southwest direction of the house.

Chapter Eleven

The

Dragon

Years of the Dragon

1904 (5/Feb/04—3/Feb/05)   1952 (5/Feb/52—3/Feb/53)
1916 (5/Feb/16—3/Feb/17)   1964 (5/Feb/64—3/Feb/65)
1928 (5/Feb/28—3/Feb/29)   1976 (5/Feb/76—3/Feb/77)
1940 (5/Feb/40—3/Feb/41)   1988 (4/Feb/88—3/Feb/89)

If you have any doubt about the classification of the 12 animal signs, or the divisions of months and years, please refer to pages xiii–xiv.

Distribution of the Stars within the Sign for 2002

Lucky Stars	Unlucky Stars
The Eight Chiefs	Isolated Living
God of Salvation	Leopard's Tail
Heavenly Salvation	Funeral Guest
	Bloody Knife
	Floating Up and Down
	Dog of Heaven

Lucky Stars
The Eight Chiefs

In the traditional Chinese ruling hierarchy, eight chiefs helped the emperor to govern the whole country. Although theoretically under the three prime ministers, they nonetheless had enough authority to keep everything in order.

When this Star appears, people will be promoted, and possess the power to rule and to scare off any challengers.

God of Salvation

Ancient Chinese peasants often led a precarious existence, vulnerable as they were to threats such as wars, floods, droughts and famines. However, they believed that in critical times the God of Salvation would protect them from total destruction.

There are three 'Salvation' Stars in the Chinese Horoscope, of which this is considered to be the most powerful. It is generally regarded as having the power to suppress negative influences from any Unlucky Stars within the same Sign.

Heavenly Salvation

'Heavenly Salvation' is one of the three Salvation Stars, which assist people in getting out of problems and disasters. Its appearance is a good omen.

When this Star appears, people have to stick to what they believe in and not give up, even if the situation appears impossible. When most needed they will get crucial assistance leading to a breakthrough.

Unlucky Stars
Isolated Living

Living alone without the care and attentions of family members was very much against the Chinese tradition. Only those who had committed wrong-doings were isolated and deserted.

The appearance of this Star is not a good omen. To maintain other people's support and friendship, try to be more open, outgoing and friendly.

Leopard's Tail

The Chinese consider leopards to be some of the fiercest animals in the jungle, who can cause a lot of trouble to those who happen to get in their way or step on their tails.

If this Star appears within the Sign it is best to be cautious, careful, discreet and maintain a low profile to avoid provoking anyone or arousing trouble.

Funeral Guest

When attending funerals in ancient China it was customary to wear white as a symbol of sadness and sobriety. Wearing red or other bright colours showed a lack of respect, and was forbidden on such sombre occasions.

This Star's appearance is a very bad omen, indicating the possibility of death among family and friends. Take extra care of older family members or anyone else who might be in danger.

Bloody Knife

Knives, and other deadly weapons, were not commonly welcomed by the ancient Chinese, who preferred to live in peace. Similarly, a bloody knife was definitely a very bad omen associated with violence and killing.

When this Star appears, it is important to maintain one's temper, and avoid quarrels and fights, which will only bring unpleasant consequences.

Floating Up and Down

The Chinese have always suffered from the periodic flooding of the Yellow River, the so-called 'Sorrow of China'. They know from experience how dangerous it is to be caught and be floating up and down in the surging current of a flooding river.

Similarly, when this Star appears, people need to stay alert during this rough year so that they won't be carried away by the swift currents, or even drowned.

Dog of Heaven

In Chinese mythology a big, fierce dog would come to threaten and eat people who had done bad deeds. Chinese mythology teaches that this creature causes the eclipse of the Sun and Moon, by swallowing either sphere. During eclipses, the people would bang cymbals or other metal objects to scare the dog and make him spit out the Sun or Moon, thus ending the eclipse.

When this Star appears, people need to stand strong and fight their opponents or they will be swallowed up.

General Overview of the Year

Although Dragons will have a lot of problems both in their business and private life this year, they shouldn't worry too much about this because they will be able to overcome most of them. This is mainly due to the appearances of the two Lucky Stars, 'God of Salvation' and 'Heavenly Salvation' within their Sign. Therefore, Dragons should stand firm and never give up at any circumstance during the year, or they will miss the sweetness of the final victory at year's end. If they really work hard enough, Dragons will have a very good chance of promotion to a much higher level, probably much higher than they might ever have expected. However, Dragons should try to be humble after success to eliminate unnecessary jealousy and attack. The best way for Dragons to handle the situation is to solidify their new foundations quietly without disturbing anyone else. The appearance of 'The Eight Chiefs' indicates that Dragons will possess the power to rule and to scare away any challenge.

Dragons won't have too much luck in money affairs this year, but they will have a satisfactory income. The appearance of the Unlucky Star 'Floating Up and Down' indicates that their fortune will fluctuate throughout the year, so that it would be much better if Dragons were more conservative about their investments. Dragons should forget about gambling or lotteries because their luck in these matters will be terrible within the year. However, Dragons have not too much to worry about their economic situation so long as they are not too greedy about money.

Dragons will have to mind their safety carefully throughout the year. The appearance of the Unlucky Star 'Bloody Knife' indicates that Dragons will be easily injured by sharp objects, so they must try to keep away from knives, saws, axes, scissors and so on. Apart from this, Dragons must take extreme care when they go swimming or fishing.

This is definitely not a romantic year for Dragons; they will be quite lonely all year round. In these circumstances, the best thing for Dragons to do is to try to be more friendly and considerate to their lover and friends.

Career	***
Money	***
Health	**
Love	*

*** = Pretty Good/** = Fair/* = Unsatisfactory

Career ***

Although Dragons will have numerous difficulties in their business, fortunately they will be able to overcome most of them without too many problems. Their strong determination at work will help them a lot in their business development. Probably, they will be promoted because of their outstanding performance, but they should try not to be blinded by that and become too proud with their co-workers. Otherwise, they will lose their support and become somewhat isolated. Dragons should never let such a terrible thing happen to them if they don't want to suffer a sudden collapse in business. Dragons must take good care of their business during the first, third, fourth, sixth and ninth months. However, they will have much better luck at work during the second, fifth, seventh and the last three months of the year. Dragons will be a sure winner if they can make good use of these months.

Money * * *

This won't be a very profitable year for Dragons. Because their fortune in money affairs will fluctuate from time to time throughout the year, Dragons should not try their luck in high-risk investments or gambling, or they will lose a lot of money. Fortunately, there will be a steady regular income for Dragons, so they don't have to worry too much about their economic situation so long as they can keep to a tight budget and not be too greedy about money. Dragons will have better luck in money affairs during the second, fifth, seventh, tenth and the last month of the year.

Health * *

The major concern of the year for Dragons is try to watch their personal safety. The appearance of the Unlucky Star 'Floating Up and Down' indicates that Dragons must take extreme care when they go swimming or fishing or engage in any other seaside activities during the third and eleventh months. Apart from this, Dragons should try to keep away from sharp objects to avoid possible injury too. Most important of all, Dragons must try not to indulge themselves in sex or alcohol too much, or their health will be seriously damaged.

Dragons have to watch the health and safety of elderly family members carefully. If anything goes wrong with them, Dragons must take them for immediate medical treatment, or they will be very sorry.

Love *

Dragons will be quite emotional and sentimental in their private life this year. It's necessary for them to control their temper and try not to let it get out of control, or their friends and lover will be scared away from them. Dragons should try to be more friendly and considerate to others if they don't want to be isolated. Dragons will have better luck in love affairs during the second, fifth, tenth and eleventh months of the year. However, they should try to improve their relationship with their lover during the first, fourth, sixth, eighth and ninth months.

Monthly In-depth Forecasts
The First Month (4 February – 5 March)

Half a loaf is better than none

Although this won't be a very good start to the year for Dragons, they should not complain too much about this. Their luck is not too bad when compared with the luck of other people around them. Dragons have to work very hard for their business during this period, but they will have a very good chance to survive. Dragons must keep in mind that they must try not to be jealous about others' success. In other words, they should be content with what they have already achieved – 'Half a loaf is better than none.' If they want to make some important changes at work, Dragons had better wait for some other time in the months to come.

Dragons should not be too greedy in money affairs. They will lose a lot of money if they risk it in high-risk investments and gambling.

Dragons will be quite emotional in love affairs. They should try to calm down and not let things get out of control. They will definitely be isolated if they are too arrogant with their friends and lover during this period.

The Second Month (6 March – 4 April)

Strike while the iron is hot

Dragons will have much better luck in business this month. Although they are still very busy at work, fortunately their efforts won't be wasted. Dragons must try to make good use of this period, and put extra effort into their business development. They must try to strike while the iron is hot. It's time for Dragons to show off their talents and capability. They will have a promotion as a consequence sooner or later. Good communication and good bargaining power will be the two big assets towards their future success in the months to come.

Dragons must have the guts to show their true feelings to their new acquaintances, or they will miss a very good chance in love. Probably, some other person will take the chance away from them.

The fortune in money affairs will be much improved for Dragons this month. They will be able to make profits from different sources during this period. But they should not let some other people fool around, or they will lose their hard-earned money.

The Third Month (5 April – 5 May)

We must learn to walk before we can run

Since the luck of Dragons will slip down from time to time this month, so they should be more cautious in handling their daily work. In other words, Dragons must try to slow their pace at work during this period, or they will have a sudden big fall.

As a matter of fact, Dragons should be more conservative in the first half of the year, and pick up momentum in the second half, because they will have much better luck at work at that time.

This is definitely not a profitable month for Dragons. They must watch their expenses carefully, and try not to let them get out of control. If somebody asks them to come in on any kind of investment, Dragons should simply say no, or they will have to say good-bye to their hard-earned cash.

The health of Dragons won't be too good during this period. They must rest and try not to exhaust themselves too much, or they will have serious health problems in the months to come. Apart from this, they should watch their safety in water, taking precautionary measures when they go fishing, swimming or diving.

The Fourth Month (6 May – 5 June)

The unexpected always happens

This is definitely one of the most unfavourable months of the year for Dragons. Different kinds of problems will arise quite suddenly during this period. Dragons will be easily defeated by their opponents if they are not well prepared psychologically beforehand. They will be in a much better position if they are able to equip themselves quite well before the thunderstorm comes. Their major concern at this critical moment is how to maintain their confidence and determination under heavy pressure. Dragons should rely on themselves and nobody else in solving their problems during this period.

A stranger will step in between Dragons and their lover this month. Gossip will make the situation even more complicated. Dragons must try to keep calm, because any irrational action will mess up the whole thing and bring nothing to them but a sad ending.

This month it won't be wise for Dragons to risk their money in either investments or gambling. They will be a sure loser if they try their luck in these matters during this period of time. Probably, there will be numerous unexpected extra expenses in the middle of the month.

The Fifth Month (6 June – 6 July)

Faith moves mountains

Dragons will have much luck in different areas this month. The heavy workload of last month will be much relieved, and they will be able to get the necessary help from colleagues and subordinates. Although Dragons will be able to overcome most difficulties at work during this period, this won't be a good time for them to carry out any new projects. They'd better wait for some other time if they want to be a sure winner at year's end. If possible, Dragons should try their best to show their faith to their clients and superiors during this period, because they will have a very good chance to win their whole-hearted support by doing so.

Without faith, Dragons will achieve nothing great this month. Dragons will have a pretty good chance in love affairs, but they will end up with nothing if they are just fooling around. They should not forget to show their faith and care to their lover.

All of a sudden, the fortune in money affairs will be much improved for Dragons. But they must try to be more conservative in handling their money affairs, because their fortune will fluctuate quite a bit this month.

The Sixth Month (7 July – 7 August)

Hasty climbers have sudden falls

Bad luck will come back to Dragons this month as suddenly as a thunderstorm. It would be much better if they didn't rush anything at this critical moment. They will be able to remain unharmed after the storm if they know how to protect themselves in a safe place. If they insist on maintaining a frantic pace during the storm, they will inevitably have a sudden big fall. And it won't be easy for them to stand up again in the months to come. Patience will help Dragons to survive when facing strong challenges at work during this period.

One thing Dragons must keep in mind is that they should not make a hasty decision in buying and selling property or stocks. If they were to do so, they would be very sorry about that in the near future.

Dragons must watch their road safety very closely this month. They must walk and drive with extreme care to ensure their personal safety.

Dragons should try not to make a hasty decision in love affairs this month, because their wit and judgement will be weakened during this period.

The Seventh Month (8 August – 7 September)

Business before pleasure

Because of the appearance of the Lucky Star 'God of Salvation' within their Sign, last month's bad luck will be gone with the wind. It's the time for Dragons to pick up their momentum again at this stage. They will face fewer obstacles at work during this period. Dragons should put extra time and effort in their career, as they will be well paid for this sooner or later. However, Dragons should try not to let their private affairs get mixed up with their business affairs. They should keep in mind that 'Business is business,' and 'Business before pleasure.'

Dragons will hurt themselves very much physically if they indulge too much in sex and alcohol. Apart from this, gossip about their romantic life will hurt their career seriously.

This will be one of the most fortunate months of the year for Dragons. It's time for them to check their budget and prepare to take action in starting a new joint venture.

The Eighth Month (8 September – 7 October)

Don't count your chickens before they are hatched

This is definitely not a profitable month for Dragons. That means, they have to be more conservative in handling their money affairs or they will lose a lot of money. It's necessary for dragons to keep their eyes wide open to watch out closely for money and business traps. If not, they will become the helpless victims of merciless cheats. Apart from this, there will be many unexpected problems one after the other during this period, so Dragons should try not to be too optimistic about their budget or investments.

Dragons will have to face numerous personal disputes at work this month. Their major concern is to try to settle them quietly and peacefully as soon as possible. They should hope for the best and prepare for the worst during this period of time.

Dragons must try to keep their promises as much as they can in love affairs this month. Otherwise they will be in big trouble or even end up with a broken relationship. Dragons will be quite emotional this month. They need to stay calm, or they might have a nervous breakdown at the end of the month.

The Ninth Month (8 October – 6 November)

Don't get mad, get even

This will be the last unfavourable month of the year for Dragons. They will face numerous challenges and unfair tricks at work. Dragons will mess up the whole thing if they lose their temper in handling these matters. Their competitors might even try to provoke them intentionally, and try to let their anger blind their wisdom. If Dragons can keep calm, they will be able to find their way out of these difficulties sooner or later. Dragons should keep in mind that their anger is just like fire and will burn down a lot of things, including themselves. Therefore, they should not get mad, but try to get even.

Dragons should not let their greediness blind them in money affairs this month. Their greediness will not only lead them to traps, but also to total financial ruin. It would not be wise for Dragons to ask for a loan this month. Their debts will drag them down all the way to the bottom.

Forgiveness will be the most effective remedy for Dragons in their private life. They should try to forget the wrongdoings of their lover and friends; if they can do so, they will receive a pleasant surprise. Conflicts and revenge will only bring misfortunes to them during this period.

The Tenth Month (7 November – 6 December)

A bird in the hand is worth two in the bush

Dragons will have pretty good luck in the last three months of the year. They will have had a very successful year overall if they can make good use of this period of time. There will be several chances knocking at their door this month, but they should not be too greedy.

Dragons should make a choice according to their own capabilities. If they go too far, they will end up with nothing. This would be a good time for Dragons to strengthen themselves through learning. A prosperous future is waiting for them if they do so.

This will be a profitable month for Dragons, but they should try to content themselves in money affairs to avoid a sudden big fall. They should keep in mind that 'A bird in the hand is worth two in the bush.'

Although Dragons will be quite popular, they should try not to fool around with too many lovers. They won't be able to make a good choice if there are too many options.

Dragons will be quite healthy this month, but they should try to watch their diet, because it will be quite easy for them to put on weight during this period.

The Eleventh Month (7 December – 5 January)

One good turn deserves another

Dragons will have lots of imagination and creative ideas at work this month. They will be very productive if they can make good use of them. But they must know how to apply their imagination and creative ideas into their daily work, or their dreams will remain just that. Apart from this, Dragons should try not to show off too much, and they should give credit to those who really deserve it. They will win the respect of those around them by doing so. As a consequence, talented people will come to work for them one after another in the near future, and this will become a great asset to their future business development.

Dragons must watch their safety when they travel. They should pay more attention to their safety in water and never try to risk their life out of a misguided sense of fun or curiosity during this period.

Dragons will enjoy a very romantic period of time this month if they are willing to show their care and tenderness to their lover. However, Dragons must try to avoid talking about politics with their friends in social gatherings, or they will be very sorry about that in the months to come.

The Twelfth Month (6 January – 3 February)

The family that prays together stays together

Dragons will be able to handle their daily work without too much difficulty this month. Their outstanding performance will be highly appreciated by their colleagues and superiors. It's time for them to get some relaxation and enjoy their success.

Dragons should reach out a helping hand to those in need. They will be handsomely rewarded for this sooner or later.

If Dragons want to carry out new projects, or to change jobs, this month would be a very good time for them to do so. Gaining the co-operation and loyalty of colleagues and subordinates is very important at this stage, because they will stick by the Dragon under any circumstances in the future.

Dragons should try to spare some more time for family members during this month. They will reach a much better understanding with each other, and this will help them to solve problems together in the rainy days to come. This will also be a priceless experience.

This will be a fortunate month in money affairs for Dragons. They will have extra income from different sources, and they will have some luck in lotteries and gambling at the end of the month.

Using Feng Shui to Improve Fortune: Directions, Colours, Numbers and Lucky Charm

The ancient Chinese used the traditional Horoscope to predict their fortune on a yearly basis – they used the art of Feng Shui to improve their luck.

It was their belief that the application of tactical Feng Shui would change their bad luck into good, and make their good luck improve even more.

This same method is still effective in today's modern world.

There are four main elements which I will use in tactical Feng Shui:

◆ Lucky Directions
◆ Lucky Colours
◆ Lucky Numbers
◆ Lucky Charm

This will be a very busy and challenging year for Dragons, so they must prepare themselves very well physically and mentally to handle these matters properly. They should stand firm and never give up under any circumstance, or they will miss the sweetness of the final victory. If they really work hard enough, Dragons will have a very good chance to be promoted to a much higher level, probably much higher than they'd ever expected. The appearance of the Lucky Star 'The Eight Chiefs' indicates that Dragons will possess the power to rule and to scare away any challenge. Unfortunately, Dragons won't have too much luck in money affairs this year, as their financial situation will fluctuate throughout the year. They must be more conservative in their investments and expenses.

Dragons must watch their safety very carefully throughout the year, and they must pay special attention to dangerous sharp objects to avoid injury.

Dragons will be quite lonely this year. The best thing for them to do is try to be more friendly and considerate to their lover and friends.

I would suggest applying the following Feng Shui tactics to improve luck so Dragons don't have to worry too much about their fate within the year.

Lucky Directions

The most favourable directions of the year for Dragons are **Southeast**, **West** and **North**. Dragons should sleep or sit in these directions if they wish to improve their fortune.

To make this procedure very simple, divide the house or room into nine imaginary squares. Then, using a compass, check the exact direction of each square as shown in Figure 11. This will help to ensure that you do not make a mistake with the direction.

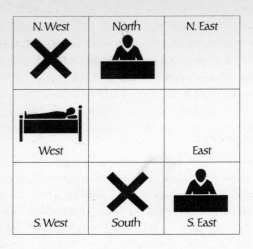

N. West	North	N. East
✕		
West		**East**
S. West	**South**	**S. East**

Figure 11

Dragons should sit in Southeast and North at work or while studying; this will ensure that their achievements are much greater than
the Stars intended. To improve health and achieve a good night's
sleep, Dragons should position the bed in the favourable direction
shown (West).

However, Dragons should try to keep away from the
unfavourable directions of the year – that is, South and Northwest,
as shown in Figure 11. Dragons should try not to sit, work or sleep
in these directions, so as to get rid of the negative influences lurking there.

Lucky Colours

According to Chinese tradition, each of the five elements has its
own representative colours. Fire is represented by red, pink and
purple, Earth by yellow and brown, and so on. As a Feng Shui

Master I would suggest **white, yellow** and **brown** as the Dragon's lucky colours for the year 2002.

Use these colours in paints, wall coverings, rugs, drapes and curtains. This will be sure to bring good fortune within the year.

However, Dragons should try not to use green, red or orange in 2002, to avoid bad luck.

Lucky Numbers

The lucky numbers for Dragons in 2002 are: **4** and **7**.

Fortune will be much improved by using these lucky numbers whenever possible. For example, if Dragons have a choice, the phone number 2477-4774 is better than 2365-8998 – because the former contains more fours and sevens, Dragon's two lucky numbers for the year.

Lucky Charm

Feng Shui Masters believe that special objects can be used as a medium between human beings and nature. The fortune of the recipient is greatly improved as the positive wave of energy from nature is passed through the object or 'lucky charm' on to the recipient.

The lucky charm for the Dragon is a pair of elephants stepping on stones with Chinese characters on them saying, 'Everything is refreshing' and 'Good luck as you wish'. There's a pearl at the tip of their raised trunks. For best results, it should be placed in the southeast direction of the house.

be quite slim. It would be much better for them to wait for another suitable period of time.

This won't be a fortunate year for Snakes, so they must watch their budgets very carefully. They should be more conservative in investments, or they will become a sure loser. Most important of all, Snakes should never try their luck in lotteries or gambling because they will probably lose much more money than they would ever have anticipated.

Because of the appearance of the two Unlucky Stars 'Illness Spell' and 'God of Death', Snakes must try to take good care of themselves. Snakes will be pretty weak both physically and mentally this year. In this situation, Snakes must try to get as much rest and sleep as they can to avoid a sudden collapse in health. If possible, Snakes should try to take a break or vacation to refresh themselves.

The love affairs of Snakes will fluctuate from time to time throughout the year, so it's necessary for them to pay special attention to improving their relationships with their lover as much as they can.

Career	*
Money	* *
Health	*
Love	* *

* * = Fair/ * = Unsatisfactory

Career *

Snakes will have to struggle very hard for their survival in business throughout the year, or they will be eliminated. Although they should try to handle their business by themselves as much as they can, their chances of success will be much improved if they are able to find a capable and sincere partner to fight together with them all the way. Snakes must handle their work with extreme care during the first, second, fourth, fifth, ninth, tenth and the last month of the year. However, they will have much better luck at work during the third, sixth and eighth months. Snakes must try to make good use of these three months if they wish to enjoy better business achievements during the year.

Money **

Snakes won't have too much luck in money affairs this year. It's necessary for them to watch their expenses and try to keep to a tight budget to avoid serious money problems. One thing Snakes must keep in mind during the year is that they should never try their luck in high-risk investments or gambling, or they will be a sure loser. Snakes must take care of their money affairs with special attention during the first, seventh, ninth and tenth months. However, they will have better luck during the third and eighth months.

Health *

Snakes will be quite weak both physically and mentally this year, so it will be necessary for them to take good care of themselves. Snakes must try to get enough rest and sleep to avoid exhaustion. Because of the appearance of the two Unlucky Stars within their Sign, Snakes would be in big trouble if they try to burn the candle at both ends. If anything goes wrong with them, Snakes should not hesitate to go to the doctor for proper medical treatment as soon as possible, because any delay would be quite dangerous. Snakes must pay special attention to their health during the first, second, fifth, ninth and the last month of the year. Apart from this, Snakes must watch their safety in water during the fourth month, and they must drive and walk with extreme care during the sixth and the last month.

Love **

This won't be a very romantic year for Snakes because their relations with their lover will fluctuate from time to time throughout the year. Unless they can do something to improve these delicate relations, their romance will fade sooner or later.

Snakes must pay more attention to their love affairs during the first, second, fifth, seventh, tenth and the last month of the year. However, they will have much better luck during the sixth, eighth and eleventh months. If possible, Snakes should try to spend more time with younger family members, and try to take good care of them.

Monthly In-depth Forecasts
The First Month (4 February – 5 March)

What goes up must come down

Because of the appearance of Unlucky Stars within their Sign, Snakes will have a pretty unlucky start to the year. They might suffer a sudden big fall in business or in money affairs. Therefore, Snakes must be very conservative in handling these two matters, or they will be a sure loser. It's better for them to curb their ambition and greediness as much as they can; modesty will be the best means to survival, not only this month, but for the rest of this year. If somebody asks a Snake to change jobs or start a new business during this period, the Snake should simply say no, or they will end up very sorry in the months to come.

No matter how busy they are, Snakes should not forget to take care of themselves, otherwise their health and safety may be endangered during this period of time. Snakes must try to keep away from dangerous heights to avoid a serious fall.

This is definitely not a romantic month for Snakes. They won't have too much luck in love affairs, and they might face a broken relationship with their lover if they are too reluctant to show their tenderness and care.

The Second Month (6 March – 4 April)

More haste, less speed

Although the luck of Snakes will improve a little bit, they will still be under heavy pressure both in business and their private life this month. Snakes should try to think carefully again and again before they take any chance in career or in financial matters. Somebody may try to push them, but Snakes should try never to make any drastic changes within this period. They should understand that everything takes time, and hasty climbers will have a sudden big fall. Most important of all, Snakes should never lose their patience in business planning and negotiation, or they will be very sorry.

If Snakes can't control their hot temper, they will be somewhat isolated by colleagues and friends. Their impatience will be the poison of their private life during this period. Snakes should walk away for a while if they find that they are losing their patience with their lover.

Snakes must try to get enough rest and sleep to avoid total exhaustion. It's very important for them to watch their diet closely, and keep away from greasy and unhealthy food.

The Third Month (5 April – 5 May)

Honesty is the best policy

Snakes will have much luck this month, so they should try to make good use of this period to improve business and financial matters. Apart from their diligence, Snakes should try to improve their relationships with colleagues, superiors and clients if they want to be more successful and productive in the months to come. Snakes should keep in mind that honesty is the best policy. Their honesty will win the whole-hearted support of others, and that will be very important for their future success or even survival. In contrast, Snakes will face a terrible ending if they try to cheat.

Snakes should not be reluctant to show their care and tenderness to their lover this month, because they will receive a nice surprise by doing so. This will be a romantic month for Snakes, and their relations with their lover will be much improved.

This will be one of the most fortunate months of the year for Snakes in money affairs. They will have extra income from different sources. And they will have luck in gambling and lotteries in the middle of the month – but they should not be too greedy.

The Fourth Month (6 May – 5 June)

Why keep a dog and bark yourself?

The luck of Snakes will slip down a little bit, so they should be more cautious in dealing with clients and competitors this month. There may be numerous difficulties and challenges at the end of the month. It will be very important for Snakes to choose a sincere partner to work with. If their partner is disloyal, they must get rid of him or her as soon as possible. Otherwise, their disloyal partner will damage them at work sooner or later. Snakes should keep in mind the motto, 'Why keep a dog and bark yourself?' Apart from this, Snakes must try to keep their eyes wide open to watch out for wicked so-called friends, and try to keep away from them. If they don't, both their business and private life will be seriously hurt.

Snakes should not talk too much about their secrets to the people around them. If they do, their secrets will be secrets no more. It will be much better if Snakes can keep away from gossip and rumours during this period.

Snakes will not have too much to worry about regarding their health, but they have to watch their safety in water, taking precautionary measures when they go swimming or diving.

The Fifth Month (6 June – 6 July)

Delays are dangerous

This is one of the most unfavourable months of the year for Snakes, so they should try to stand up firmly at work for themselves. They have to put extra time and effort into their daily work during this period. It's necessary for Snakes to finish their work as soon as possible, because any delay will be dangerous. Probably, their enemies will make use of this opportunity to attack them. If Snakes are able to take action before their enemies, then they will be in a much better situation. Snakes will be bothered by numerous personal disputes at the beginning of the month, and they should try to settle these at once, or there will be endless trouble in the months to come.

Snakes should not be reluctant to say sorry to their lover and friends this month for their wrongdoings. Their delay in making apologies will leave them quite embarrassed.

The health of Snakes will be quite weak this month. In case anything goes wrong with them, they should go to see a doctor for medical treatment as soon as possible. Apart from this, they have to take good care of their children when at playgrounds or country parks.

The Sixth Month (7 July – 7 August)

Opportunity never knocks twice at any man's door

Snakes will have much better luck this month, so they should try to take advantage of as many opportunities as they can, because opportunity never knocks twice. They will be very sorry if they miss these good chances. If somebody asks them along on a joint venture during this period, Snakes should consider it very carefully, because it may prove very successful and profitable. Snakes should try to contact clients directly and try to understand their real interests; this will be very important to their future success. This would be a good time for Snakes to strengthen themselves through study. It's never too late to learn.

The health of Snakes will be much improved this month. However, they should try to watch their road safety in the middle of the month. Apart from this, Snakes should not indulge themselves too much in alcohol.

Snakes will have pretty good luck in love affairs, but they should not be reluctant to show their love and care to their loved ones, or they will miss a very good chance. Apart from this, they should keep an ear out for those delicate hints from their loved ones.

The Seventh Month (8 August – 7 September)

Do right and fear no man

Snakes will face certain difficulties at work this month, and that will make them very busy during this period of time. They must have the guts to take responsibility with confidence, or they will be badly beaten. Determination and confidence will be the two important keys for career survival. As long as they are doing right, Snakes should fear no man, including their superiors. However, they should try to keep within the law, because it would be quite easy to get involved in legal problems or even end up in gaol if they were to commit any wrongdoing. As a matter of fact, Snakes will be able to overcome most of their difficulties if they dare to face them without fear.

The fortune in money affairs will fluctuate from time to time for Snakes. In this situation, they should be more conservative in handling financial matters. Apart from this, they should try to keep their eyes wide open for money traps.

Snakes must have the guts to show their determination in love affairs, or their loved ones will be gone with the wind during this period of time. They should keep in mind the motto, 'Faint heart never won fair lady.'

The Eighth Month (8 September – 7 October)

He that would eat the fruit must climb the tree

Snakes will become very active in both their business and private life this month. They will find out that the more they work, the more they earn during this period of time. It's very important for Snakes to fight for themselves, because there will be no one to depend on at work. If Snakes wish to realize important achievements in their career, they should try to make good use of this month or they will become a sure loser at the end of the year.

Snakes should not be afraid to take calculated risks this month, because they will have pretty good luck for the time being. Snakes must watch the quality control of their products if they want to reach a better market. This will be a very good time for Snakes to develop their business in foreign places.

This month, Snakes will have good fortune in money affairs. If they are applying for a loan, they will be approved. And they will be pretty lucky in gambling, but they should become more cautious near the end of the month.

Snakes will be quite popular during this period. However, they should not indulge themselves too much in love affairs, and try not to let private matters mess up their career.

The Ninth Month (8 October – 6 November)

It is easier to pull down than to put up

Bad luck will come as suddenly as a thunderstorm for Snakes this month, so they must try to be more conservative in handling their business and financial matters. This is the period of time that Snakes have to think about how to survive instead of expanding. That means Snakes should think about how to protect themselves and how to preserve their hard-earned rewards. They will meet with numerous obstacles on their way to success if they start new projects during this period. It would be much safer for Snakes to try to slow their pace and hide themselves from the thunderstorm for the time being. To make the situation even worse, Snakes will find out that their colleagues and friends will turn a cold shoulder when they ask for help.

Snakes must try to get enough rest and sleep in order to avoid total exhaustion. Apart from this, they should try to stay away from crowded places and filthy food. It is very important for them to have the necessary injections before they go abroad.

This is definitely not a profitable month for Snakes. They must try to cut back on their extravagant habits, and try to save as much as they can for the rainy days to come. Gambling will lead Snakes to total destruction, so they'd better forget about it during this period of time.

The Tenth Month (7 November – 6 December)

When the cat's away, the mice will play

The business life of Snakes will be in a big mess this month if they fail to organize their daily work according to a good plan. Their contracts may be cancelled, proposals may be denied and their schedules may be interrupted during this period of time. Therefore, Snakes should keep their eyes wide open to detect any possible trouble before it gets out of control. If possible, Snakes should not leave their post, because when the cat's away, the mice will play. Everything will be messed up when they come back. They might even lose their job.

Snakes have to watch out for strangers trying to step in between their lover and them. If this happens, they should face the challenge and not hide their heads in the sand. They will be a sure loser if they do so.

Again, Snakes won't have good luck in money affairs this month. They would lose a lot of money if they try their luck in high-risk investments or gambling. Apart from this, they must make sure that the windows and doors of their houses and offices are securely locked to avoid a burglary or break-in.

The Eleventh Month (7 December – 5 January)

Easy come, easy go

Although the luck of Snakes will improve a little bit, they still have to work hard for their career survival this month. However, they should not work too hard or burn the candle at both ends, or their health will be in big trouble. Snakes must try not to give up at this stage, otherwise their previous efforts will have been wasted. Snakes will have much better luck at work in the coming new year, so it's necessary for them to struggle on at this critical moment. A good partner will help them out of trouble during this period. Therefore, it's very important for Snakes to find and keep a good partner for their future development.

Snakes will have some luck in money affairs this month. Unfortunately, their money will be easy come, easy go. Unless Snakes can handle their money with extreme care, and try to keep to a very tight budget, they will end up with nothing after all.

This will be a romantic month for Snakes, but they should try not to fool around, or both their career and health will be spoiled. If Snakes fail to keep their hot temper under control, their new acquaintances will walk away from them sooner or later.

The Twelfth Month (6 January – 3 February)

Don't change horses mid-stream

The last month of the year won't be a favourable period of time for Snakes, so they have to take good care of their business and health. Snakes should stay at their post and stand firm in their career. They will lose a lot of ground to their competitors if they make any drastic change in their business at this stage. Snakes should keep in mind that they should never change horses mid-stream. Otherwise, many unexpected challenges will arise, and lead them along the road of destruction. Probably, Snakes will be confused at work, so they should ask for professional advice and guidance from experts before they make any important decision for their future development.

Unless Snakes can keep to a healthy diet, their health will be seriously jeopardized. Their major concern this month is their health and safety. It's necessary for Snakes to see a doctor as soon as there is any sign that something might be the matter with them. Apart from this, they must drive with extreme care at night at the beginning of the month.

Snakes will be quite lonely this month. Although they may be surrounded by several admirers, it will be quite impossible for Snakes to have a close relationship with them. Other than that, Snakes should try not to criticize their friends during this period, or they will be very sorry about that in the near future.

Using Feng Shui to Improve Fortune: Directions, Colours, Numbers and Lucky Charm

The ancient Chinese used the traditional Horoscope to predict their fortune on a yearly basis – they used the art of Feng Shui to improve their luck.

It was their belief that the application of tactical Feng Shui would change their bad luck into good, and make their good luck improve even more.

This same method is still effective in today's modern world.

There are four main elements which I will use in tactical Feng Shui:

◆ Lucky Directions
◆ Lucky Colours
◆ Lucky Numbers
◆ Lucky Charm

Snakes will have a pretty rough year in 2002, so it's necessary for them to struggle very hard for survival in business. And they will have no one to rely on except themselves during their long struggle at work. It would be much better if Snakes could try to keep a low profile and mind their own business. However, a capable and sincere partner will help Snakes a lot in improving their situation. If possible, Snakes should not try to carry out any important projects this year.

This won't be a fortunate year for Snakes, so they must keep their eyes wide open to watch their budget. Most important of all, Snakes must try not to risk their hard-earned money in gambling.

Snakes will be quite weak physically and mentally, so it will be necessary for them to try to get as much rest and sleep as they can.

Snakes won't have too much luck in love affairs, and they should therefore try to improve their relationships with their lover with patience and care.

I would suggest applying the following Feng Shui tactics to improve luck so Snakes don't have to worry too much about their fate within the year.

Lucky Directions

The most favourable directions of the year for Snakes are **Southwest**, **West** and **Northeast**. Snakes should sleep or sit in these directions if they wish to improve their fortune.

To make this procedure very simple, divide the house or room into nine imaginary squares. Then, using a compass, check the exact direction of each square as shown in Figure 12. This will help to ensure that you do not make a mistake with the direction.

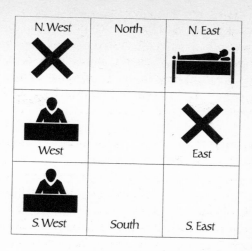

N. West	North	N. East
✗		🛏
👤 West		✗ East
👤 S. West	South	S. East

Figure 12

Snakes should sit in Southwest and West at work or while studying; this will ensure that their achievements are much greater than
the Stars intended. To improve health and achieve a good night's
sleep, Snakes should position the bed in the favourable direction
shown (Northeast).

However, Snakes should try to keep away from the
unfavourable directions of the year – that is, East and Northwest,
as shown in Figure 12. Snakes should try not to sit, work or sleep
in these directions, so as to get rid of the negative influences lurking there.

Lucky Colours

According to Chinese tradition, each of the five elements has its
own representative colours. Fire is represented by red, pink and
purple, Earth by yellow and brown, and so on. As a Feng Shui

Master I would suggest **blue**, **grey** and **red** as Snake's lucky colours for the year 2002.

Use these colours in paints, wall coverings, rugs, drapes and curtains. This will be sure to bring good fortune within the year.

However, Snakes should try not to use brown or white in 2002, to avoid bad luck.

Lucky Numbers

The lucky numbers for Snakes in 2002 are: **2** and **6**.

Fortune will be much improved by using these lucky numbers whenever possible. For example, if Snakes have a choice, the phone number 2266-6226 is better than 2779-6688 – because the former contains more twos and sixes, Snake's two lucky numbers for the year.

Lucky Charm

Feng Shui Masters believe that special objects can be used as a medium between human beings and nature. The fortune of the recipient is greatly improved as the positive wave of energy from nature is passed through the object or 'lucky charm' on to the recipient.

The lucky charm for the Snake in 2002 is a pair of phoenixes, each embracing a huge gold ingot. The phoenix is a very rare auspicious bird in Chinese folklore, which wouldn't rest on ordinary places to downgrade itself. A huge gold ingot, because of its great value, is a worthy place for the phoenix to rest itself. This lucky charm means 'to embrace fortune securely'. For best results, this lucky charm should be put in the west direction of the house.

Day-by-day Analysis of Luck

Do the right thing at the right time every day

The charts that appear on pages 228–333 relate particularly to the art of perfect timing. The principle of daily forecasting or Chinese 'date-choosing' stems from the belief that there is a time and a place for everything. The ancient Chinese believed that certain things were particularly suited to certain days. The calculation and application of this becomes the framework for date-choosing.

Through their observations, the ancient Chinese realized that different kinds of plants need different climates to grow, and that they had to follow nature's rules if they were to have a good harvest. For them, it therefore followed that a single day cannot be suitable for *all* tasks and activities. Thus, people have to choose a suitable day to do their jobs if they want to achieve good results.

The calculation involved in date-choosing can seem complicated, but fortunately there are some traditional Feng Shui rules that make things easier. The calculation is based mainly on the distribution of the different Stars on different days. Because this distribution changes from day to day, the suitable activities also change accordingly.

Format

The format of these forecast charts (which run from 30 December 2001 to 31 December 2002) is as follows:

The first two columns list the **Date** and **Day of the week**.

The third column lists the **Favourable Activities** for that day. Days highlighted in ★ indicate a very fortunate day; those with a • indicate a fair-to-middling day; those with ♦ indicate an unlucky day. Try not to schedule important activities for unlucky days; however, if you cannot avoid doing a certain job on an unlucky day, choose the **Lucky Hours** of that day (column four). This alternative is sometimes quite effective. Neither are all hours suitable, even on a generally very fortunate day. Choosing the lucky hours for a task or project can add to the effect of a fortuitous day, while less lucky hours can undermine this effect.

The ancient Chinese believed there were good directions and bad directions, and that these changed on a daily basis. The three most important were the **Direction of Happiness** (column five), the **Direction of Wealth** (column six) and the **Direction of Opportunity** (column seven).

The Direction of Happiness is an auspicious pointer for seating plans at weddings, birthday parties, etc., to ensure happiness for all participants.

If looking for good investments or good income, sitting in the Direction of Wealth on a given day will enhance your efforts.

If looking for promotion or a breakthrough in your career or in your studies, sitting in the Direction of Opportunity for a given day will foster success.

Most important of all, there will be some brief forecasts for individual Signs under the chart, so that readers can know what they are going to face during that particular period of time when using the charts. This will prove to be a very helpful supplement to the 'Monthly In-depth Forecasts' of the Signs in previous chapters.

Explanations

The 32 activities listed are divided into seven categories:

◆ Spiritual Rites
◆ Social Interactions
◆ Out and About
◆ Commercial Activities
◆ Cleaning
◆ Household Activities
◆ Outdoor Pursuits

Spiritual Rites
(1) Worship

The ancient Chinese used to worship different kinds of gods and spirits. For instance, they would worship the Gods of heaven, the Gods of nature, and the honorable dead such as the historical figures and their ancestors. In order to purify themselves before the gods or honorable dead, they would not eat any meat nor take any wine for a period of time, and would take a bath shortly before the worship ceremony. According to the Chinese tradition, there were certain days especially suitable for worship.

(2) Blessing

The ancient Chinese would go to the temples and ask the monks there to perform the blessing ceremony for them when they were experiencing troubles over a period of time. They hoped that their luck would change from bad to good as a result. In order to have a better result, they would choose a suitable day for blessing.

There is a big difference between 'Blessing' and 'Worship'. The former refers to the blessing of the living people, while the latter refers to the memorial ceremony for the gods or the honorable dead.

(3) Burial

The ancient Chinese believed that whether the newly dead were buried properly or not would have strong influences over the fate of their descendants. As a result, they would sincerely ask the Feng Shui Masters to choose a good place and good timing to bury their newly dead family member. They considered that the burial timing must be right, or the Feng Shui of the grave would be minimized.

According to the Chinese tradition, there were some days especially suitable for burial of the dead. Not only the living descendants would be benefited, but also the buried dead could rest peacefully in the grave as a result.

Social Interactions

(4) Engagement

The procedures of an ancient Chinese marriage were very complicated and tediously long. From engagement to wedding would take months or even years. The parents of the young couple would insist that both engagement and wedding should take place on lucky days to ensure a happy ending and a fruitful marriage with many offspring. During the engagement, the parents of both families had to exchange gifts as a sign of commitment to one another.

(5) Wedding

The meaning of marriage in ancient China was quite different from that of nowadays. The ancient Chinese marriage was considered to be the tool of reproduction so that the family could keep on growing from generation to generation. The emphasis of an ancient marriage was on reproduction rather than on true love between the young man and woman.

The parents would therefore choose a lucky day for the wedding ceremony of their youngsters, to ensure as many descendants as possible. Date-choosing for weddings has remained a primary concern in Chinese society over the centuries.

(6) Social Gathering

Friendship and harmonious relationships were highly appreciated in ancient China. People would choose a lucky day to meet their new and old friends. They would clean themselves and prepare gifts before the meeting to show their sincerity. They believed that there would be a happy gathering, mutual understanding and agreement as a result.

This can apply to formal and informal social gatherings of different natures, such as birthday parties, fund-raising events, exhibitions and conferences in the modern society.

(7) Start Learning

The ancient Chinese would study very hard to pass the Civil Examination, because they could change their social status from the common class to the ruling class after they performed well. Parents would urge their youngsters to go to school at an early age. The 'Start Learning' ceremony was one of the most important events in a person's life, because not too many people would have the chance to receive an education. The ceremony was very serious and would be performed only on the lucky day, to ensure the success in the future examination.

Nowadays this can also apply to starting different kinds of lessons, such as in driving, dancing, singing and so on.

Out and About
(8) Moving

The ancient Chinese were very reluctant to move house, either to move to a new home or a new town, because they were afraid to give up the old and start all over in a new place. In order to increase their confidence, they would choose a lucky day for moving. They believed that this would make their new lives easier and smoother.

(9) Travelling

The ancient Chinese used to bind themselves to their cultivated lands because all their wealth, property and relatives were closely connected with their lands. As a result, they were very reluctant to travel. Besides which, the traffic systems were not well developed at the time, so that travelling would be quite uncomfortable and dangerous. If they had to travel, they would choose a lucky day to start their journey. They hoped that a good beginning would bring a good ending.

Commercial Activities
(10) Grand Opening

The ancient Chinese merchants would choose a very lucky day for the grand opening of their shops in order to have a good beginning of their business. Usually, firecrackers and the lion dance would be used during the ceremony to bring good luck to the shop.

Nowadays, the moment of ribbon-cutting and champagne-toasting should take place at the lucky hour of the lucky day, to ensure a successful venture.

(11) Signing Contracts

Even in ancient China it was the norm for contracts to be drawn up and signed to confirm any business or legal transactions. In order to avoid argument and conflicts in the future, the parties involved would choose a lucky day to sign these contracts.

This can apply to the signing of different kinds of commercial and legal documents in the modern world.

(12) Trading

Commercial activities were not common in ancient China, nor were well appreciated. However, different kinds of trading would take place in different ways, such as trading of crops, domestic animals, fields and houses. Both the buyer and the seller would choose a lucky day for trading in order to bring about the greatest possible mutual benefit.

This can apply to the trading of different kinds of business in the modern world. People can earn more profit if they pick a lucky day for their trading, according to traditional Chinese beliefs.

[13] Money Collecting

The ancient Chinese considered that money in the market was similar to fish in the river: neither was easy to catch. Just as the fishermen would wait for the right tide to catch fish, the Chinese would choose the right timing to collect money. If they chose the wrong time to do so, then they would not only have difficulties in collecting money, but also would have difficulties keeping hold of it.

Cleaning

[14] House Cleaning

The ancient Chinese considered that the house of a family was equivalent to the body of a person. Both should be kept clean at all times, or disease and bad luck would ensue.

People would go to the doctor and clear up the accumulated toxic deposits inside the body when they were sick. In much the same way, people would choose a lucky day to clean their homes thoroughly when they had been experiencing bad luck over a period of time. They hoped that their bad luck would be swept away with the dirt from their homes.

[15] Bathing

The meaning of 'bath' in the Chinese date-choosing was quite different from that of the daily bath in the modern world. In ancient times, the Chinese would clean themselves thoroughly before important ceremonies to show their purity and sincerity. They would carefully choose a suitable day to take this ritual bath. In addition, some would keep to a vegetarian diet for a period of time in order to purify their bodies completely inside and out.

If they had been experiencing bad luck for a period of time, they would add some kind of herbs to the bath water to wash away the bad luck.

(16) Hair Cutting

The ancient Chinese had a very strong feeling about their hair because it was regarded as a symbol of their ego. Without a proper hairstyle, it was felt they would lose all sense of self and self-esteem. History tells us that thousands and thousands of Chinese were killed by a new ruler between 1644 and 1645 simply because they refused to cut their hair.

The ancient Chinese believed that to cut hair on lucky days for this activity would bring good luck.

(17) Tailoring

The ancient Chinese of the common class had few clothes because they couldn't afford them. They would have clothes made for them only for very special occasions, such as weddings, birthdays and New Year's Day. They would choose a lucky day to have fittings at the tailor because they believed that this would bring good luck to them.

Household Activities

(18) Bed Set-up

The main entrance, stove and sleeping bed are considered the three essential factors in Feng Shui studies. Therefore, to set up a bed in the proper place at the proper time in a new house is a prime concern of the Feng Shui Master. If it is done properly, the person who sleeps in the bed will enjoy good sleep and, consequently, good health.

If people wanted to get a new bed but the Feng Shui Master was not available to help them, they would choose a lucky day from the calendar to do so.

(19) Stove Set-up

The stove (cooker) is considered important because it is closely related to the health of the whole family. According to Feng Shui theory, if the stove is set up in the wrong place of the kitchen, the food prepared in it will spoil the health of the family members.

(20) Door Fixing

The ancient Chinese used to pay special attention to the main entrance of their homes because of security and Feng Shui reasons. They considered that a pair of sturdy doors at the main entrance, acting as the main gate to guard them from being attacked by robbers and gangsters, were of primary importance. They also considered that if the door at the main entrance opened in the right direction to let the good *Chi* (positive energy) flow into the house, the Feng Shui of that house would be greatly enhanced. No matter the reasons, they would choose a lucky day to fix the door at their main entrance.

(21) Crack Refilling

The ancient Chinese considered that the small cracks and large holes that appear in walls and anywhere else in the home or workplace should be filled in as soon as possible. This stemmed in part from practical reasons: if there were no holes, then no rats, snakes or poisonous insects or animals could live there. The work usually involved using cement and different herbs to fill up the cracks and holes. They would choose a suitable day to do this kind of work, but not necessarily a very lucky day.

(22) Wall Decorating

The ancient Chinese considered the wall of a house to be as important as the face of a human being. If there were some cracks or dirt on the wall, that meant the owner lost 'face'. They would hire workers to repair and redecorate in a suitable fashion. They believed that their luck would be changed after that.

This can apply to decorating with paint or wallpaper. It is also applicable to the practice of tearing down old walls and building new ones.

(23) Construction

The ancient Chinese would break the ground of a site at the beginning of each new construction. In order to please the guardian spirits of the earth, they would kill a rooster and pig as sacrifices to the spirits as part of the ground-breaking ceremony. The ceremony had to take place at the lucky hour of the lucky day to ensure the safety of the new structure. The ancient Chinese deeply believed that to break the ground at the wrong time would lead to many problems and accidents during construction.

(24) Ditching

The ancient Chinese villagers used to dig ditches in and out of their cultivated-lands and houses for irrigation and washing. They would carefully choose the right direction in which to dig the ditches, at the right time, in order to let the good Chi flow in together with the water. According to Feng Shui theory, the water should flow in from the good direction and flow out towards the bad direction.

This can apply to any piping or plumbing work in the modern houses. The building of a pond or swimming pool is another modern-day example.

(25) Passage Fixing

The passages of a house were considered to be as important as the blood vessels of a human body. Therefore, good maintenance of the passages were necessary in order to keep good Feng Shui. If there was any damage, then it would be fitting to repair it as soon as possible. The ancient Chinese believed that to change a rough passage into a smooth one would change their luck from bad to good. People would choose a lucky day for fixing passages in and out of their homes.

(26) Nursery Set-up

To have more offspring in order to increase the family was the prime concern of the ancient Chinese. Therefore, they would be very serious about choosing a lucky day to set up a nursery room for their baby. They believed that a good nursery set-up would bring a healthy baby with good fortune.

This can also be applied to the set-up of a cot or Moses basket for a newborn baby.

Outdoor Pursuits

(27) Hunting

Hunting was not very common in ancient China because it was the privilege of the nobility. But gradually the common people would go hunting on a much smaller scale on some special occasions. In order to ensure a safe and productive hunt, they would choose a lucky day to go hunting.

(28) Capturing

According to Chinese tradition, there was a difference between hunting and catching. Hunting involved killings with weapons, while catching referred to catching animals and birds alive with nets or traps. The former was the privilege of the nobility, while the latter was a common practice among the lower classes.

(29) Planting

The ancient Chinese paid special attention to planting because agriculture was their major source of income. Besides the plantation of major crops, they would have some other crops to supplement their income. They believed that the harvest of any crop would be determined by the day on which it was planted. If they didn't choose the right timing, then their harvest would be spoiled.

This can also apply to the planting of flowers and fruit trees on a smaller scale. The plants will grow much better if a suitable day for planting is chosen according to the classic Chinese calendar.

(30) Animal Acquiring

The ancient Chinese farmers would raise some animals and fowl such as pigs, sheep, ducks and chickens to supplement their incomes. Because infections were very common among these kinds of domestic creatures, the farmers had to be very cautious about raising them. When they wanted to bring in some new animals, they would choose a lucky day to do so. They believed that an unlucky day would bring in bad luck together with the animals, especially in the form of infections and disease.

This can apply to the buying of small domestic pets, such as cats, dogs, rabbits, gerbils, canaries, budgerigars, etc. To buy these pets or to accept them as gifts on a lucky day is believed to ensure their healthy growth, and also a close relationship between the animals and the owners.

(31) Fishing

Chinese fishermen used to go out to the open sea for fishing with sampans or junks. These small wooden boats were not strong enough for the rough sea. Any accidents could happen suddenly. They might end up losing their boats or even their lives.

In order to avoid these kinds of tragedies, the fishermen would set up strict rules to be followed among themselves; choosing a lucky day for fishing was one of them. They believed that this would bring them back safely with abundance of fish.

This also applies to angling in any form.

(32) Net Weaving

Fishermen used nets to catch fish in the water, while 'capturers' used nets to trap animals in the forest. Therefore, nets were very important in the ancient Chinese villages. Both the fishermen and capturers would take good care of their nets. They would choose a lucky day to prepare new nets or to repair the old ones.

This can apply to the preparation of objects that are similar to nets, such as fences, drapes and curtains.

Date	Day	Favourable Activities
Dec 30	Sun	• Passage Fixing, Wall Decorating
31	Mon	★ Construction, Animal Acquiring, Engagement, Blessing, Trading, Signing Contracts, Wedding
Jan 1	Tue	• Nursery Set-up, Worship, Capturing, Hunting
2	Wed	◆ Unlucky Day Not suitable for important activities
3	Thu	• Hunting
4	Fri	★ Social Gathering, Wedding, Trading, Grand Opening, Moving, Travelling, Start Learning, Burial
5	Sat	• Hair Cutting, House Cleaning, Capturing, Bathing

★ Lucky Day   • Ordinary Day   ◆ Unlucky Day

Lucky Hours	Direction of Happiness	Direction of Wealth	Direction of Opportunity
03-05 13-15	S	W	NW
01-03 05-07 09-11 13-15 15-17 17-19	SE	N	NE
23-01 03-05 13-15 15-17	NE	N	SW
01-03 03-05 13-15 15-17 17-19	NW	E	SW
03-05 05-07 09-11 15-17	SW	E	S
23-01 01-03 05-07 07-09 09-11 13-15 17-19	S	S	E
23-01 01-03 03-05 07-09 09-11 15-17	SE	S	SE

Horse – It's time to carry out new projects. *Pig* – You have to work hard for your survival. *Mouse* – Be aware, your over-confidence will blind you. *Snake* – If possible, better not to ask for a loan. *Rooster* – Diligence is the mother of good fortune. *Sheep* – Try to get as much rest and sleep as possible.

Date	Day	Favourable Activities
Jan 6	Sun	• Worship, Money Collecting, Capturing, Hunting
7	Mon	◆ Unlucky Day Not suitable for important activities
8	Tue	◆ Unlucky Day Not suitable for important activities
9	Wed	• Worship, Signing Contracts
10	Thu	★ Moving, House Cleaning, Engagement, Bathing, Bed Set-up, Stove Set-up
11	Fri	★ Grand Opening, Net Weaving, Money Collecting, Engagement, Blessing, Start Learning
12	Sat	• Wall Decorating, Worship

★ Lucky Day   • Ordinary Day   ◆ Unlucky Day

Lucky Hours			Direction of Happiness	Direction of Wealth	Direction of Opportunity
01-03	03-05	05-07	NE	SE	NE
09-11					
23-01	01-03	03-05	NW	SE	SW
05-07					
23-01	01-03	09-11	SW	W	W
17-19	19-21				
23-01	09-11	11-13	S	W	NW
17-19					
01-03	05-07	07-09	SE	N	NE
09-11	11-13				
23-01	03-05	05-07	NE	N	SW
11-13					
01-03	03-05	07-09	NW	E	NE
09-11	11-13				

Dragon – Try to pay your bills as soon as possible. *Tiger* – Your romance will turn over a new leaf. *Dog* – Watch your diet to avoid infections. *Monkey* – Not a good time to try your luck at gambling. *Ox* – What goes up must come down. *Rabbit* – It's time to improve your relationship with your important clients.

Date	Day	Favourable Activities
Jan 13	Sun	★ Moving, Construction, Animal Acquiring, Blessing, Trading, Signing Contracts
14	Mon	★ Hair Cutting, Capturing, Hunting, Bathing, Bed Set-up
15	Tue	◆ Unlucky Day Not suitable for important activities
16	Wed	★ Grand Opening, Moving, Construction, Stove Set-up, Travelling, Burial
17	Thu	★ Wedding, Grand Opening, Construction, Engagement, Trading, Signing Contracts, Travelling, Burial
18	Fri	• Worship
19	Sat	◆ Unlucky Day Not suitable for important activities

★ Lucky Day   • Ordinary Day   ◆ Unlucky Day

Lucky Hours			Direction of Happiness	Direction of Wealth	Direction of Opportunity
01-03 03-05 09-11 11-13 19-21			SW	E	NE
01-03 03-05 05-07 09-11			S	S	E
23-01 03-05 05-07 09-11 11-13 19-21			SE	S	E
23-01 01-03 07-09 09-11 15-17 17-19			NE	SE	SW
23-01 01-03 03-05 07-09 15-17 17-19			NW	SE	SW
23-01 03-05 05-07 09-11 15-17 17-19 19-21			SW	W	W
01-03 03-05 11-13 17-19 19-21			S	W	W

Snake – Try to reach out a helping hand to those in need. *Rooster* – You will have some luck in lotteries and gambling. *Monkey* – Better try to keep to a tight budget to avoid money problems. *Mouse* – Don't let your ambitions go beyond your ability. *Pig* – Watch out, there will be several unexpected expenses at the weekend.

Date	Day	Favourable Activities
Jan 20	Sun	• Tailoring, Worship, Bathing, Bed Set-up
21	Mon	• Tailoring, Worship
22	Tue	★ Wedding, Moving, Construction, Planting, Engagement, Trading, Signing Contracts, Burial
23	Wed	★ Grand Opening, Worship, Bed Set-up, Burial, Stove Set-up, Travelling
24	Thu	• Capturing, Burial
25	Fri	★ Social Gathering, Moving, Trading, Construction, Money Collecting, Engagement, Signing Contracts
26	Sat	★ Worship, Hair Cutting, House Cleaning, Hunting, Bathing

★ Lucky Day   • Ordinary Day   ◆ Unlucky Day

Lucky Hours	Direction of Happiness	Direction of Wealth	Direction of Opportunity
01-03 05-07 07-09 09-11 15-17 17-19	SE	N	NE
23-01 03-05 05-07 09-11 15-17 17-19	NE	N	N
01-03 03-05 05-07 07-09	NW	E	NE
03-05 05-07 09-11 11-13 19-21	SW	E	NE
01-03 03-05 05-07 09-11 17-19	S	S	E
23-01 05-07 07-09 09-11 15-17 19-21	SE	S	SE
01-03 03-05 17-19	NE	SE	SW

Ox – Keep a low profile and mind your own business. *Sheep* – The darkest hour is just before dawn. *Dog* – You must have the guts to face any challenge. *Horse* – Stop playing with fire in love affairs. *Rabbit* – You never miss water until the well runs dry. *Dragon* – Try to take a break or vacation to refresh yourself.

Date	Day	Favourable Activities
Jan 27	Sun	◆ Unlucky Day Not suitable for important activities
28	Mon	★ Grand Opening, Hair Cutting, Construction, Animal Acquiring, Planting, Hunting, Start Learning, Burial
29	Tue	★ Wedding, Grand Opening, Moving, Construction, Trading, Travelling, Start Learning, Burial
30	Wed	● Worship, Capturing
31	Thu	◆ Unlucky Day Not suitable for important activities
Feb 1	Fri	● Tailoring, Worship, Burial
2	Sat	★ Worship, Engagement, Blessing, Bed Set-up

★ Lucky Day   ● Ordinary Day   ◆ Unlucky Day

Lucky Hours	Direction of Happiness	Direction of Wealth	Direction of Opportunity
23-01 03-05 05-07 15-17 19-21	NW	SE	SW
23-01 01-03 09-11 15-17 17-19 19-21	SW	W	W
01-03 11-13 17-19	S	W	NW
01-03 05-07 11-13 15-17	SE	N	NE
23-01 03-05 05-07 11-13 15-17	NE	N	SW
01-03 15-17 17-19	NW	E	NE
01-03 03-05 05-07 09-11 11-13 15-17	SW	E	NE

Tiger – Watch the health of elderly family members. *Rooster* – You will gain nothing without sweat. *Snake* – Half a loaf is better than none. *Mouse* – Pay more attention to economic developments in your business. *Pig* – You must have the guts to make revolutionary changes at work.

Date	Day	Favourable Activities
Feb 3	Sun	◆ Unlucky Day Not suitable for important activities
4	Mon	★ Hair Cutting, House Cleaning, Engagement, Trading, Signing Contracts, Travelling
5	Tue	• Tailoring, Net Weaving, Worship, Blessing
6	Wed	• Passage Fixing
7	Thu	★ Wedding, Grand Opening, Construction, Engagement, Bed Set-up, Door Fixing, Burial, Trading
8	Fri	★ Moving, Worship, Construction, Animal Acquiring, Blessing, Travelling, Burial
9	Sat	◆ Unlucky Day Not suitable for important activities

★ Lucky Day   • Ordinary Day   ◆ Unlucky Day

Lucky Hours			Direction of Happiness	Direction of Wealth	Direction of Opportunity
01-03 03-05 05-07 19-21			S	S	E
23-01 03-05 05-07 19-21			SE	S	E
01–03 03-05 07-09 13-15 17-19 21-23			NE	SE	SW
01-03 17-19 19-21			NW	SE	N
09-11 11-13 17-19 19-21 21-23			SW	W	NW
09-11 11-13 13-15 17-19 21-23			S	W	NW
01-03 07-09 09-11 13-15			SE	N	SW

Monkey – Drive carefully at night. *Dragon* – Try not to be too greedy in money affairs. *Ox* – Every man is the architect of his own fortune. *Horse* – Better not to cheat your lover during this period. *Dog* – Watch your valuables to avoid a burglary. *Sheep* – Be humble, because pride goes before a fall.

Date	Day	Favourable Activities
Feb 10	Sun	★ Worship, Hair Cutting, House Cleaning, Fishing, Bathing, Burial
11	Mon	• Start Learning
12	Tue	Chinese New Year
13	Wed	◆ Unlucky Day Not suitable for important activities
14	Thu	• Bed Set-up, Stove Set-up
15	Fri	• Social Gathering, Animal Acquiring, Trading, Signing Contracts
16	Sat	★ Social Gathering, Hair Cutting, Engagement, Bathing, Trading, Signing Contracts

★ Lucky Day   • Ordinary Day   ◆ Unlucky Day

Lucky Hours	Direction of Happiness	Direction of Wealth	Direction of Opportunity
07-09 09-11 11-13 13-15	NE	N	SW
01-03 11-13 13-15	NW	E	SW
01-03 03-05 05-07 11-13 13-15 19-21	SW	E	S
01-03 03-05 05-07 07-09 09-11 13-15	S	S	E
01-03 07-09 09-11 17-19 19-21	SE	S	E
03-05 07-09 13-15 17-19 19-21	NE	SE	NE
03-05 05-07 13-15 19-21 21-23	NW	SE	NE

Rabbit – Try not to indulge yourself too much in sex and alcohol.
Mouse – Watch your diet carefully to avoid digestive diseases.
Rooster – Living without an aim is like sailing without a compass.
Snake – Keep away from dangerous heights. *Tiger* – Try to keep silent, because the walls have ears.

Date	Day	Favourable Activities
Feb 17	Sun	★ Wedding, Grand Opening, Moving, Worship, Construction, Blessing, Travelling, Burial
18	Mon	• Passage Fixing, Worship
19	Tue	★ Wedding, Grand Opening, Moving, Construction, Engagement, Trading, Travelling, Burial
20	Wed	• Worship, Capturing, Fishing, Start Learning
21	Thu	◆ Unlucky Day Not suitable for important activities
22	Fri	• Worship, Blessing
23	Sat	◆ Social Gathering, Grand Opening, Construction, Blessing, Trading, Signing Contracts, Start Learning, Burial

★ Lucky Day   • Ordinary Day   ◆ Unlucky Day

Lucky Hours	Direction of Happiness	Direction of Wealth	Direction of Opportunity
09-11 17-19 21-23	SW	W	W
01-03 09-11 11-13 13-15 17-19 19-21	S	W	W
05-07 09-11 13-15 17-19	SE	N	SW
03-05 05-07 09-11 11-13 13-15	NE	N	SW
01-03 07-09 09-11 11-13 13-15	NW	E	SW
03-05 07-09 09-11 11-13	SW	E	NE
03-05 05-07 09-11 13-15 19-21 21-23	S	S	E

Pig – Try not to indulge yourself too much in sex and alcohol. *Snake* – Try to curb your ambition and greed to avoid a sudden big fall. *Ox* – It's time to think about future planning. *Sheep* – Listen to the opinions of experts in business and investments. *Monkey* – If necessary, don't be shy to ask for help.

Date	Day	Favourable Activities
Feb 24	Sun	• Worship, Capturing, Hunting, Bathing
25	Mon	◆ Unlucky Day Not suitable for important activities
26	Tue	• Net Weaving, Worship
27	Wed	★ Social Gathering, Animal Acquiring, Engagement, Signing Contracts, Trading, Burial
28	Thu	★ Wedding, Grand Opening, Moving, Worship, Construction, Trading, Travelling, Burial
Mar 1	Fri	• Social Gathering, Tailoring, Net Weaving, Worship
2	Sat	• Passage Fixing, Wall Decorating

★ Lucky Day   • Ordinary Day   ◆ Unlucky Day

Lucky Hours			Direction of Happiness	Direction of Wealth	Direction of Opportunity
03-05	05-07	07-09	SE	S	E
11-13	19-21	21-23			
01-03	03-05	07-09	NE	SE	NE
13-15					
01-03	03-05	05-07	NW	SE	N
17-19					
05-07	11-13	17-19	SW	W	W
03-05	11-13	13-15	S	W	NW
01-03	05-07	09-11	SE	N	NE
13-15	17-19				
03-05	11-13	13-15	NE	N	SW

Horse – Make hay while the sun shines. *Dog* – The more you work, the more you get. *Tiger* – Try to save more money for some unexpected expenses. *Mouse* – When in Rome, do as the Romans do. *Rabbit* – It's a good time to carry out new projects. *Rooster* – Watch your safety in water. *Snake* – No pain, no gain.

Date	Day	Favourable Activities
Mar 3	Sun	★ Social Gathering, Wedding, Worship, Grand Opening, Moving, Trading, Travelling, Burial
4	Mon	★ Wedding, Moving, Worship, Construction, Animal Acquiring, Planting, Travelling, Burial
5	Tue	◆ Unlucky Day Not suitable for important activities
6	Wed	◆ Unlucky Day Not suitable for important activities
7	Thu	★ Wedding, Grand Opening, Moving, Construction, Bed Set-up, Trading, Travelling, Burial
8	Fri	★ Tailoring, Moving, Construction, Net Weaving, Animal Acquiring, Travelling, Start Learning
9	Sat	◆ Unlucky Day Not suitable for important activities

★ Lucky Day   • Ordinary Day   ◆ Unlucky Day

Lucky Hours			Direction of Happiness	Direction of Wealth	Direction of Opportunity
01-03 03-05 11-13 13-15 17-19			NW	E	SW
03-05 05-07 09-11 11-13			SW	E	S
01-03 05-07 07-09 09-11 13-15 17-19			S	S	E
01-03 03-05 07-09 09-11 15-17			SE	S	SE
01-03 03-05 05-07 09-11 13-15			NE	SE	NE
01-03 03-05 05-07 13-15			NW	SE	SW
01-03 09-11 19-21 21-23			SW	W	W

Dragon – Strike while the iron is hot. *Pig* – Try to keep the faith at work. *Monkey* – Try to get as much rest and sleep as you can. *Ox* – Don't hesitate to start a new project. *Sheep* – Take care of your business by yourself. *Tiger* – Co-operation will achieve more than competition with your opponents.

Date	Day	Favourable Activities
Mar 10	Sun	★ Nursery Set-up, Wedding, Ditching, Moving, Construction, Travelling, Animal Acquiring, Engagement
11	Mon	★ Crack Refilling, Tailoring, Net Weaving, Trading, Signing Contracts
12	Tue	• Worship, House Cleaning, Hunting, Bathing
13	Wed	• Hair Cutting, House Cleaning, Bathing, Travelling
14	Thu	★ Social Gathering, Grand Opening, Net Weaving, Worship, Money Collecting, Trading
15	Fri	• Passage Fixing, Wall Decorating
16	Sat	★ Wedding, Worship, Construction, Trading, Signing Contracts, Grand Opening, Burial

★ Lucky Day   • Ordinary Day   ◆ Unlucky Day

Lucky Hours	Direction of Happiness	Direction of Wealth	Direction of Opportunity
09-11 11-13 21-23	S	W	NW
01-03 05-07 07-09 09-11 11-13 13-15	SE	N	NE
03-05 05-07 11-13 13-15	NE	N	SW
01-03 03-05 07-09 09-11 11-13 13-15 21-23	NW	E	NE
01-03 03-05 09-11 11-13 13-15 19-21	SW	E	NE
01-03 03-05 05-07 09-11 13-15 21-23	S	S	E
03-05 05-07 09-11 11-13 19-21	SE	S	E

Snake – Try not to make any drastic changes, or you will be sorry. *Mouse* – If you play with fire, you get burned. *Dog* – You have to try your best to keep your promises. *Rooster* – If possible, try to take a break or vacation to refresh yourself. *Dragon* – It's time to show off your talent and capabilities to earn a promotion.

Date	Day	Favourable Activities
Mar 17	Sun	★ Worship, House Cleaning, Capturing, Bathing, Start Learning
18	Mon	◆ Unlucky Day Not suitable for important activities
19	Tue	★ Tailoring, Worship, Capturing, Hunting, Fishing
20	Wed	★ Social Gathering, Grand Opening, Moving, Engagement, Blessing, Trading, Travelling, Start Learning
21	Thu	◆ Unlucky Day Not suitable for important activities
22	Fri	★ Wedding, Grand Opening, Moving, Hair Cutting, Construction, Engagement, Travelling, Start Learning
23	Sat	★ Tailoring, Money Collecting, Planting, Trading, Signing Contracts

★ Lucky Day   • Ordinary Day   ◆ Unlucky Day

Lucky Hours			Direction of Happiness	Direction of Wealth	Direction of Opportunity
01-03 07-09 09-11 13-15 15-17			NE	SE	SW
01-03 03-05 07-09 15-17			NW	SE	SW
03-05 05-07 09-11 15-17 19-21 21-23			SW	W	W
01-03 03-05 11-13 13-15 19-21 21-23			S	W	W
01-03 05-07 07-09 09-11 15-17			SE	N	NE
03-05 05-07 09-11 15-17			NE	N	N
01-03 03-05 05-07 07-09			NW	E	NE

Sheep – Try to be more serious at work. *Tiger* – Better try to pick up momentum again, or you will be left far behind. *Monkey* – Improve your communications and relationships with clients. *Pig* – Try to cut your extravagant habits. *Dragon* – Keep alert to avoid money traps. *Ox* – Watch out for the safety of young children.

Date	Day	Favourable Activities
Mar 24	Sun	• Trading, Signing Contracts, Travelling, Social Gathering
25	Mon	• Hair Cutting, House Cleaning, Travelling
26	Tue	★ Social Gathering, Grand Opening, Money Collecting, Blessing, Trading, Signing Contracts
27	Wed	• Passage Fixing, Wall Decorating
28	Thu	★ Social Gathering, Tailoring, Worship, Money Collecting, Blessing
29	Fri	• Net Weaving, House Cleaning, Fishing, Travelling
30	Sat	◆ Unlucky Day Not suitable for important activities

★ Lucky Day   • Ordinary Day   ◆ Unlucky Day

Lucky Hours	Direction of Happiness	Direction of Wealth	Direction of Opportunity
03-05 05-07 09-11 11-13 19-21	SW	E	NE
01-03 03-05 05-07 09-11 21-23	S	S	E
05-07 07-09 09-11 15-17 19-21	SE	S	SE
01-03 03-05 13-15	NE	SE	SW
05-07 07-09 15-17 19-21 21-23	NW	SE	SW
01-03 09-11 13-15 15-17 19-21 21-23	SW	W	W
01-03 11-13 13-15 21-23	S	W	NW

Dog – Try to keep a tight budget to avoid financial problems. *Sheep* – Watch out for a possible robbery. *Mouse* – Don't try your luck at investments or gambling. *Rabbit* – Keep a low profile and avoid gossip. *Rooster* – Human pride is human weakness. *Snake* – Don't try to rush yourself in business matters.

Date	Day	Favourable Activities
Mar 31	Sun	• Bed Set-up, Stove Set-up, Trading, Fishing
Apr 1	Mon	★ Grand Opening, Moving, Construction, Planting, Trading, Signing Contracts, Travelling, Start Learning
2	Tue	◆ Unlucky Day Not suitable for important activities
3	Wed	• Net Weaving, Worship, Animal Acquiring, Start Learning
4	Thu	★ Tailoring, Construction, Trading, Signing Contracts, Burial
5	Fri	• Crack Refilling
6	Sat	• Worship

★ Lucky Day   • Ordinary Day   ◆ Unlucky Day

Lucky Hours	Direction of Happiness	Direction of Wealth	Direction of Opportunity
01-03 05-07 11-13 13-15 15-17	SE	N	NE
03-05 05-07 11-13 13-15 15-17	NE	N	SW
01-03 13-15 15-17	NW	E	NE
01-03 03-05 05-07 09-11 11-13 15-17 21-23	SW	E	NE
01-03 03-05 05-07 13-15 19-21	S	S	E
03-05 05-07	SE	S	E
01-03 03-05 07-09 13-15 17-19 21-23	NE	SE	SW

Tiger – You will have some luck at lotteries and gambling. *Horse* – Try not to challenge or provoke your superiors. *Pig* – Mutual trust with your lover will be very important at this stage. *Monkey* – Health is wealth. *Dragon* – Good communication and bargaining power are very important assets towards your success.

Date	Day	Favourable Activities
Apr 7	Sun	• Hair Cutting, House Cleaning, Bathing, Stove Set-up
8	Mon	• Worship
9	Tue	• Passage Fixing, Wall Decorating
10	Wed	• House Cleaning, Animal Acquiring, Bathing, Door Fixing
11	Thu	★ Wedding, Net Weaving, Worship, Hair Cutting, Animal Acquiring, Fishing, Bathing, Burial
12	Fri	◆ Unlucky Day Not suitable for important activities
13	Sat	◆ Unlucky Day Not suitable for important activities

★ Lucky Day   • Ordinary Day   ◆ Unlucky Day

Lucky Hours			Direction of Happiness	Direction of Wealth	Direction of Opportunity
01-03	15-17	17-19	NW	SE	N
09-11 11-13 15-17 17-19 21-23			SW	W	NW
09-11 11-13 13-15 17-19 21-23			S	W	NW
01-03 07-09 09-11 13-15 15-17			SE	N	SW
07-09 09-11 11-13 13-15 15-17			NE	N	SW
01-03 11-13 13-15 15-17			NW	E	SW
01-03 03-05 05-07 11-13 13-15			SW	E	S

Ox – Watch out for the danger of fire both at home and at work.
Sheep – A compromise is much better than a humiliating defeat.
Rabbit – It's time to look for a potential partner for your future
development. *Dog* – A bad penny always turns up. *Rooster* – Watch
out for your road and water safety on Friday and Saturday.

Date	Day	Favourable Activities
Apr 14	Sun	◆ Unlucky Day Not suitable for important activities
15	Mon	• Worship, Animal Acquiring, Capturing, Hunting
16	Tue	★ Ditching, Grand Opening, Moving, Construction, Planting, Trading, Signing Contracts, Travelling
17	Wed	• Crack Refilling, Worship
18	Thu	• Worship
19	Fri	★ Wedding, Grand Opening, Moving, Construction, Money Collecting, Planting, Engagement, Trading
20	Sat	• Social Gathering, Grand Opening, Net Weaving, Worship

★ Lucky Day   • Ordinary Day   ◆ Unlucky Day

Lucky Hours			Direction of Happiness	Direction of Wealth	Direction of Opportunity
01-03	03-05	05-07	S	S	E
07-09	09-11	13-15			
01-03	07-09	09-11	SE	S	E
15-17	17-19				
03-05	07-09	13-15	NE	SE	NE
17-19					
03-05	05-07	13-15	NW	SE	SW
15-17	21-23				
09-11	15-17	17-19	SW	W	W
21-23					
01-03	09-11	11-13	S	W	W
13-15	17-19				
05-07	09-11	13-15	SE	N	SW
15-17	17-19				

Snake – Your relationship with your lover will be much improved.
Mouse – Keep your windows and doors securely locked to avoid
burglary or robbery. *Tiger* – Don't put all your eggs in one basket. *Pig*
– You will be easily cheated if you are too greedy about money.
Monkey – Take challenges bravely, or you will miss chances.

Date	Day	Favourable Activities
Apr 21	Sun	• Net Weaving, Hair Cutting
22	Mon	• Worship, House Cleaning, Animal Acquiring, Bathing
23	Tue	★ Hair Cutting, Animal Acquiring, Capturing, Bathing, Burial
24	Wed	◆ Unlucky Day Not suitable for important activities
25	Thu	• Net Weaving, Bathing
26	Fri	◆ Unlucky Day Not suitable for important activities
27	Sat	• Money Collecting, Animal Acquiring, Capturing, Fishing

★ Lucky Day   • Ordinary Day   ◆ Unlucky Day

Lucky Hours			Direction of Happiness	Direction of Wealth	Direction of Opportunity
03-05	05-07	09-11	NE	N	SW
11-13	13-15	15-17			
01-03	07-09	09-11	NW	E	SW
11-13	13-15	15-17			
03-05	07-09	09-11	SW	E	NE
11-13					
03-05	05-07	09-11	S	S	E
13-15	21-23				
03-05	05-07	07-09	SE	S	E
11-13	21-23				
01-03	03-05	07-09	NE	SE	NE
13-15	15-17				
01-03	03-05	05-07	NW	SE	N
15-17	17-19				

Horse – There's no such thing as a free lunch. *Dragon* – You must learn to walk before you can run. *Ox* – Try to settle personal disputes as soon as possible. *Monkey* – Don't be shy about showing tenderness and care towards your loved ones. *Rabbit* – Fairly and softly go far in a day. *Dog* – Stand firm and refuse to give up.

Date	Day	Favourable Activities
Apr 28	Sun	★ Social Gathering, Grand Opening, Moving, Construction, Engagement, Trading, Travelling, Start Learning
29	Mon	★ Crack Refilling, Tailoring, Worship, Stove Set-up
30	Tue	● Wall Decorating, Tailoring
May 1	Wed	★ Bathing, House Cleaning, Worship, Social Gathering
2	Thu	● Worship
3	Fri	● Wall Decorating, Passage Fixing
4	Sat	● Burial, Bathing, House Cleaning, Worship

★ Lucky Day   ● Ordinary Day   ◆ Unlucky Day

Lucky Hours	Direction of Happiness	Direction of Wealth	Direction of Opportunity
05-07 11-13 17-19	SW	W	W
03-05 11-13 13-15	S	W	NW
01-03 05-07 09-11 13-15 15-17 17-19	SE	N	NE
03-05 11-13 13-15 15-17	NE	N	SW
01-03 03-05 11-13 13-15 15-17 17-19	NW	E	SW
03-05 05-07 09-11 11-13 15-17	SW	E	S
01-03 05-07 07-09 09-11 13-15 17-19	S	S	E

Pig – There is always a first time. *Horse* – Try to have more enthusiasm at work. *Mouse* – Watch your expenses, or your money will be 'easy come, easy go'. *Monkey* – Forgiveness is very important in your private life. *Snake* – You will be in big trouble if you try to break any laws or regulations.

Date	Day	Favourable Activities
May 5	Sun	★ Fishing, Animal Acquiring, Hair Cutting, Worship, Wedding, Burial
6	Mon	• Wedding, Worship, Hair Cutting, Capturing
7	Tue	◆ Unlucky Day Not suitable for important activities
8	Wed	◆ Unlucky Day Not suitable for important activities
9	Thu	★ Travelling, Signing Contracts, Trading, Engagement, Animal Acquiring, Construction, Grand Opening
10	Fri	• Fishing, Capturing
11	Sat	• Start Learning, Travelling, Worship, Social Gathering

★ Lucky Day   • Ordinary Day   ◆ Unlucky Day

Lucky Hours			Direction of Happiness	Direction of Wealth	Direction of Opportunity
01-03 03-05 07-09 09-11 15-17			SE	S	SE
01-03 03-05 05-07 09-11 13-15			NE	SE	NE
01-03 03-05 05-07 13-15			NW	SE	SW
01-03 09-11 17-19 19-21			SW	W	W
09-11 11-13 17-19			S	W	NW
01-03 05-07 07-09 09-11 11-13 13-15			SE	N	NE
03-05 05-07 11-13 13-15			NE	N	SW

Tiger – Better try to keep your temper in love affairs. *Rooster* – It's a suitable time to buy property and valuables. *Dragon* – Try to keep your confidence and determination under pressure. *Ox* – Try to make good use of your imagination and creativity. *Snake* – Why keep a dog and bark yourself?

Date	Day	Favourable Activities
May 12	Sun	★ Worship, Construction, Trading, Signing Contracts, Travelling, Burial
13	Mon	★ Wedding, Tailoring, Moving, Animal Acquiring, Engagement, Blessing
14	Tue	★ Grand Opening, Worship, Blessing, Hair Cutting, House Cleaning, Construction, Travelling, Burial
15	Wed	● Worship
16	Thu	● Bathing, House Cleaning, Worship, Passage Fixing
17	Fri	★ Wedding, Grand Opening, Moving, Construction, Trading, Signing Contracts, Travelling, Burial
18	Sat	● Capturing, Hair Cutting, Worship, Social Gathering

★ Lucky Day   ● Ordinary Day   ◆ Unlucky Day

Lucky Hours	Direction of Happiness	Direction of Wealth	Direction of Opportunity
01-03 03-05 07-09 09-11 11-13 13-15	NW	E	NE
01-03 03-05 09-11 11-13 13-15 19-21	SW	E	NE
01-03 03-05 05-07 09-11 13-15	S	S	E
03-05 05-07 09-11 11-13 19-21	SE	S	E
01-03 07-09 09-11 13-15 15-17 17-19	NE	SE	SW
01-03 03-05 07-09 15-17 17-19	NW	SE	SW
03-05 05-07 09-11 15-17 17-19 19-21	SW	W	W

Dog – You can't get blood from a stone. *Rabbit* – Sex and alcohol will hurt your health seriously. *Mouse* – Don't turn a cold shoulder to your new acquaintances. *Sheep* – Better try to get someone to share your burden. *Pig* – It's better to be safe than sorry. *Snake* – Try to keep away from wicked so-called friends to avoid legal wrangles.

Date	Day	Favourable Activities
May 19	Sun	◆ Unlucky Day Not suitable for important activities
20	Mon	◆ Unlucky Day Not suitable for important activities
21	Tue	★ Grand Opening, Animal Acquiring, Planting, Engagement, Trading, Travelling, Start Learning, Burial
22	Wed	★ Wedding, Moving, Animal Acquiring, Engagement, Signing Contracts, Travelling, Trading, Burial
23	Thu	★ Wedding, Grand Opening, Worship, Construction, Planting, Trading, Travelling, Start Learning
24	Fri	● Net Weaving, Hunting
25	Sat	● Social Gathering, Tailoring

★ Lucky Day   ● Ordinary Day   ◆ Unlucky Day

Lucky Hours	Direction of Happiness	Direction of Wealth	Direction of Opportunity
01-03 03-05 11-13 13-15 17-19 19-21	S	W	W
01-03 05-07 07-09 09-11 15-17 17-19	SE	N	NE
03-05 05-07 09-11 15-17 17-19	NE	N	N
01-03 03-05 05-07 07-09	NW	E	NE
03-05 05-07 09-11 11-13 19-21	SW	E	NE
01-03 03-05 05-07 09-11 17-19	S	S	E
05-07 07-09 09-11 15-17 19-21	SE	S	SE

Dragon – You will be a sure loser if you try your luck at gambling. *Monkey* – It takes all sorts to make a world. *Ox* – You will get a promotion very soon. *Snake* – Try not to keep your business secret. *Rooster* – Fine feathers make fine birds. *Tiger* – Try to pay your bills at once to avoid endless trouble.

Date	Day	Favourable Activities
May 26	Sun	★ Wedding, Moving, House Cleaning, Animal Acquiring, Engagement, Blessing, Travelling, Burial
27	Mon	• Worship, House Cleaning
28	Tue	★ Wedding, Grand Opening, Moving, Construction, Engagement, Door Fixing, Signing Contracts, Travelling
29	Wed	★ Travelling, Signing Contracts, Trading, Construction, Moving, Grand Opening, Wedding, Burial
30	Thu	★ Blessing, Planting, Construction, Hair Cutting, Moving, Wedding
31	Fri	◆ Unlucky Day Not suitable for important activities
Jun 1	Sat	◆ Unlucky Day Not suitable for important activities

★ Lucky Day   • Ordinary Day   ◆ Unlucky Day

Lucky Hours			Direction of Happiness	Direction of Wealth	Direction of Opportunity
01-03	03-05	13-15	NE	SE	SW
17-19					
03-05	05-07	15-17	NW	SE	SW
19-21					
01-03	09-11	13-15	SW	W	W
15-17	17-19	19-21			
01-03	11-13	13-15	S	W	NW
17-19					
01-03	05-07	11-13	SE	N	NE
13-15	15-17				
03-05	05-07	11-13	NE	N	SW
13-15	15-17				
01-03	13-15	15-17	NW	E	NE
17-19					

Mouse – Try to cheer your feelings of loneliness. *Rabbit* – The better the day, the better the deed. *Pig* – Don't take part in any joint ventures at this stage. *Horse* – Dress yourself up to win a fair lady. *Dog* – Better take a break or vacation. *Sheep* – Put extra time and effort in at work to overcome difficulties.

Date	Day	Favourable Activities
Jun 2	Sun	★ Wedding, Grand Opening, Construction, Planting, Trading, Travelling, Start Learning, Burial
3	Mon	• Net Weaving, Capturing
4	Tue	• Start Learning, Stove Set-up, Worship, Social Gathering
5	Wed	• Stove Set-up, Tailoring, Crack Refilling
6	Thu	• Tailoring, Crack Refilling
7	Fri	• Worship
8	Sat	★ Travelling, Door Fixing, Moving, Money Collecting, Construction, Tailoring, Grand Opening, Wedding

★ Lucky Day   • Ordinary Day   ◆ Unlucky Day

Lucky Hours	Direction of Happiness	Direction of Wealth	Direction of Opportunity
01-03 03-05 05-07 09-11 11-13 15-17	SW	E	NE
01-03 03-05 05-07 13-15 19-21	S	S	E
03-05 05-07 19-21	SE	S	E
01-03 03-05 07-09 13-15 17-19	NE	SE	SW
01-03 15-17 17-19 19-21	NW	SE	N
09-11 11-13 15-17 17-19 19-21 21-23	SW	W	NW
09-11 11-13 13-15 17-19 21-23	S	W	NW

Ox – Cheer up, love makes the world go around. *Snake* – Work promptly, any delay will be dangerous. *Rooster* – Take it easy, don't go beyond your abilities at work. *Tiger* – Lend your money and lose your friend. *Dog* – Wait for a suitable time to express yourself. *Dragon* – Any irrational action will mess up your relationship with your lover.

Date	Day	Favourable Activities
Jun 9	Sun	★ Wall Decorating, Wedding, Moving, Grand Opening, Tailoring, Construction, Blessing, Travelling
10	Mon	★ Bathing, House Cleaning, Worship, Hair Cutting, Wall Decorating, Passage Fixing
11	Tue	◆ Unlucky Day Not suitable for important activities
12	Wed	◆ Unlucky Day Not suitable for important activities
13	Thu	◆ Unlucky Day Not suitable for important activities
14	Fri	• Worship
15	Sat	★ Start Learning, Signing Contracts, Trading, Animal Acquiring, Construction, Grand Opening

★ Lucky Day   • Ordinary Day   ◆ Unlucky Day

Lucky Hours	Direction of Happiness	Direction of Wealth	Direction of Opportunity
01-03 07-09 09-11 13-15 15-17	SE	N	SW
07-09 09-11 11-13 13-15 15-17	NE	N	SW
01-03 11-13 13-15 15-17	NW	E	SW
01-03 03-05 05-07 11-13 13-15 19-21	SW	E	S
01-03 03-05 05-07 07-09 09-11 13-15	S	S	E
01-03 07-09 09-11 15-17 17-19 19-21	SE	S	E
03-05 07-09 13-15 17-19 19-21	NE	SE	NE

Mouse – You need a good plan, or you will gain nothing after a hard struggle. *Monkey* – Keep your eyes wide open to possible dangers. *Pig* – A bird in the hand is worth two in the bush. *Horse* – Try to improve your relationship with the people around you. *Rabbit* – Try to be honest, because cheats never prosper.

Date	Day	Favourable Activities
Jun 16	Sun	• Worship, Net Weaving
17	Mon	★ Travelling, Bed Set-up, Engagement, Construction, Moving, Wedding, Nursery Set-up
18	Tue	• Tailoring, Crack Refilling
19	Wed	• Worship
20	Thu	★ Moving, House Cleaning, Construction, Planting, Trading, Signing Contracts, Travelling
21	Fri	★ Travelling, Blessing, Construction, Hair Cutting, Moving, Tailoring, Grand Opening, Burial
22	Sat	• House Cleaning, Hair Cutting, Wall Decorating, Passage Fixing

★ Lucky Day   • Ordinary Day   ◆ Unlucky Day

Lucky Hours	Direction of Happiness	Direction of Wealth	Direction of Opportunity
03-05 05-07 13-15 17-19 19-21	NW	SE	SW
09-11 15-17 17-19 21-23	SW	W	W
01-03 09-11 11-13 13-15 17-19 19-21	S	W	W
05-07 09-11 13-15 15-17 17-19	SE	N	SW
03-05 05-07 09-11 11-13 13-15 15-17	NE	N	SW
01-03 07-09 09-11 11-13 13-15 15-17	NW	E	SW
03-05 07-09 09-11 11-13	SW	E	NE

Dog – You will meet with splendid achievements at work if you try hard enough. *Sheep* – Variety is the spice of life. *Dragon* – You will become quite popular. *Tiger* – Out of debt, out of trouble. *Snake* – Don't hesitate to take chances. *Ox* – Watch your expenses, or they will get out of control.

Date	Day	Favourable Activities
Jun 23	Sun	★ Signing Contracts, Trading, Blessing, Tailoring, Wedding
24	Mon	• Bathing, Worship
25	Tue	◆ Unlucky Day Not suitable for important activities
26	Wed	• Worship, Hair Cutting
27	Thu	★ Wedding, Grand Opening, Construction, Engagement, Trading, Travelling, Start Learning, Burial
28	Fri	• Worship
29	Sat	★ Nursery Set-up, Social Gathering, Tailoring, Moving, Planting, Engagement, Travelling, Start Learning

★ Lucky Day   • Ordinary Day   ◆ Unlucky Day

Lucky Hours	Direction of Happiness	Direction of Wealth	Direction of Opportunity
03-05 05-07 09-11 13-15 19-21 21-23	S	S	E
03-05 05-07 07-09 11-13 19-21 21-23	SE	S	E
01-03 03-05 07-09 13-15 15-17	NE	SE	NE
01-03 03-05 05-07 15-17 17-19	NW	SE	N
05-07 11-13 17-19	SW	W	W
03-05 11-13 13-15	S	W	NW
01-03 05-07 09-11 13-15 15-17 17-19	SE	N	NE

Rooster – Pay more attention to the quality control of your products. *Mouse* – Be careful, watch out for falling objects. *Pig* – You can't win them all. *Rabbit* – Mutual trust with your lover is necessary at this stage. *Horse* – Don't burn the candle at both ends. *Monkey* – Watch out, there's no smoke without fire.

Date	Day	Favourable Activities
Jun 30	Sun	★ Crack Refilling, Tailoring, Worship, Planting
Jul 1	Mon	• Wall Decorating
2	Tue	★ Construction, Trading, Travelling, Moving, Grand Opening, Wedding, Social Gathering, Burial
3	Wed	★ Travelling, Burial, Construction, Hair Cutting, Moving, Grand Opening
4	Thu	• House Cleaning, Hair Cutting, Wall Decorating, Passage Fixing
5	Fri	★ Signing Contracts, Trading, Blessing, Construction, Grand Opening, Wedding, Social Gathering
6	Sat	• Start Learning, Bathing, Capturing, Worship

★ Lucky Day   • Ordinary Day   ◆ Unlucky Day

Lucky Hours	Direction of Happiness	Direction of Wealth	Direction of Opportunity
03-05 11-13 13-15 15-17	NE	N	SW
01-03 03-05 11-13 13-15 15-17 17-19	NW	E	SW
03-05 05-07 09-11 11-13 15-17	SW	E	S
01-03 05-07 07-09 09-11 13-15 17-19	S	S	E
01-03 03-05 07-09 09-11 15-17	SE	S	SE
01-03 03-05 05-07 09-11 13-15	NE	SE	NE
01-03 03-05 05-07 13-15	NW	SE	SW

Tiger – Concentrate only on the job in hand at this stage. *Dog* – Spend more time with your family in your leisure time. *Snake* – Hurry up, take action before your opponents do. *Sheep* – It's time for you to make revolutionary changes. *Ox* – Better be humble enough to avoid the jealousy of hidden enemies.

Date	Day	Favourable Activities
Jul 7	Sun	◆ Unlucky Day Not suitable for important activities
8	Mon	◆ Unlucky Day Not suitable for important activities
9	Tue	★ Grand Opening, Tailoring, Engagement, Bed Set-up, Trading, Signing Contracts, Travelling
10	Wed	★ Travelling, Planting, Construction, Animal Acquiring, Worship, Moving, Grand Opening, Wedding
11	Thu	● Worship, Money Collecting, Planting, Capturing
12	Fri	● Start Learning
13	Sat	● Net Weaving, Burial

★ Lucky Day   ● Ordinary Day   ◆ Unlucky Day

Lucky Hours	Direction of Happiness	Direction of Wealth	Direction of Opportunity
01-03 09-11 17-19 19-21 21-23	SW	W	W
09-11 11-13 17-19 21-23	S	W	NW
05-07 07-09 09-11 11-13 13-15	SE	N	NE
03-05 05-07 11-13 13-15	NE	N	SW
03-05 07-09 09-11 11-13 13-15 21-23	NW	E	NE
03-05 09-11 11-13 13-15 19-21	SW	E	NE
03-05 05-07 09-11 13-15 21-23	S	S	E

Dragon – Don't make a hasty decision about buying or selling property. *Rooster* – Bad money drives out good. *Mouse* – It's time to build up a better relationship with important clients. *Horse* – Better to diversify your investments. *Pig* – The new broom sweeps clean. *Rabbit* – Save more money for the rainy days to come.

Date	Day	Favourable Activities
Jul 14	Sun	• Travelling, Worship, Wedding, Social Gathering
15	Mon	★ Wedding, Grand Opening, Moving, Hair Cutting, Construction, Signing Contracts, Travelling, Burial
16	Tue	• Bathing, House Cleaning, Worship, Burial
17	Wed	• Fishing, Hunting, Worship, Net Weaving
18	Thu	★ Bathing, Animal Acquiring, Construction, Tailoring, Social Gathering
19	Fri	◆ Unlucky Day Not suitable for important activities
20	Sat	◆ Unlucky Day Not suitable for important activities

★ Lucky Day   • Ordinary Day   ◆ Unlucky Day

Lucky Hours	Direction of Happiness	Direction of Wealth	Direction of Opportunity
03-05 05-07 09-11 11-13 19-21	SE	S	E
07-09 09-11 13-15 15-17 17-19	NE	SE	SW
03-05 07-09 15-17 17-19	NW	SE	SW
03-05 05-07 09-11 15-17 17-19 19-21 21-23	SW	W	W
03-05 11-13 13-15 17-19 19-21 21-23	S	W	W
05-07 07-09 09-11 15-17 17-19	SE	N	NE
03-05 05-07 09-11 15-17 17-19	NE	N	N

Monkey – Try to eat a well-balanced diet. *Tiger* – Don't turn down the offer of help, or you will be sorry later on. *Snake* – Opportunity never knocks twice at any man's door. *Dog* – Your anger will bring nothing to you but destruction. *Ox* – Old habits die hard. *Sheep* – Where there's a will, there's a way.

Date	Day	Favourable Activities
Jul 21	Sun	★ Signing Contracts, Trading, Bed Set-up, Engagement, Planting, Grand Opening, Social Gathering, Burial
22	Mon	★ Start Learning, Travelling, Signing Contracts, Trading, Moving, Construction, Grand Opening, Wedding
23	Tue	• Capturing, Planting, Animal Acquiring, Worship
24	Wed	• Start Learning, Door Fixing, Worship, Social Gathering
25	Thu	★ Worship, Tailoring, Crack Refilling, Burial
26	Fri	★ Travelling, Bed Set-up, Engagement, Animal Acquiring, Worship, Wedding
27	Sat	★ Door Fixing, Planting, Construction, House Cleaning, Hair Cutting, Worship

★ Lucky Day   • Ordinary Day   ◆ Unlucky Day

Lucky Hours	Direction of Happiness	Direction of Wealth	Direction of Opportunity
03-05 05-07 07-09	NW	E	NE
03-05 05-07 09-11 11-13 19-21	SW	E	NE
03-05 05-07 09-11 17-19 21-23	S	S	E
05-07 07-09 09-11 15-17 19-21	SE	S	SE
03-05 13-15 17-19	NE	SE	SW
03-05 05-07 15-17 19-21 21-23	NW	SE	SW
09-11 13-15 15-17 17-19 19-21 21-23	SW	W	W

Horse – Try not to show off too much in love affairs. *Pig* – Be more friendly and sincere, or you will be isolated. *Rabbit* – Of two evils, choose the lesser. *Mouse* – Be more considerate to the people around you. *Dragon* – Hasty climbers have sudden falls. *Rooster* – You must know how to protect yourself at work.

Date	Day	Favourable Activities
Jul. 28	Sun	★ Door Fixing, Bed Set-up, Blessing, Animal Acquiring, Burial
29	Mon	• Worship, Net Weaving
30	Tue	★ Signing Contracts, Trading, Engagement, Planting, Construction, Animal Acquiring, Social Gathering
31	Wed	◆ Unlucky Day Not suitable for important activities
Aug 1	Thu	◆ Unlucky Day Not suitable for important activities
2	Fri	★ Grand Opening, Construction, Bed Set-up, Travelling, Start Learning, Burial
3	Sat	★ Wedding, Grand Opening, Moving, Construction, Burial, Trading, Signing Contracts, Travelling

★ Lucky Day   • Ordinary Day   ◆ Unlucky Day

Lucky Hours	Direction of Happiness	Direction of Wealth	Direction of Opportunity
11-13 13-15 17-19 21-23	S	W	NW
05-07 11-13 13-15 15-17	SE	N	NE
03-05 05-07 11-13 13-15 15-17	NE	N	SW
13-15 15-17 17-19	NW	E	NE
03-05 05-07 09-11 11-13 15-17 21-23	SW	E	NE
03-05 05-07 13-15 19-21	S	S	E
03-05 05-07 19-21	SE	S	E

Tiger – It's not easy to maintain a relationship with your loved ones at this stage. *Sheep* – Try to pay your bills as soon as possible. *Dog* – Double-check your work to avoid careless mistakes. *Snake* – Keep away from drugs and alcohol. *Ox* – Not a good time for investments or carrying out new projects.

Date	Day	Favourable Activities
Aug 4	Sun	★ Social Gathering, Wedding, Tailoring, Moving, Construction, Planting, Travelling, Burial
5	Mon	• Start Learning, Stove Set-up, Worship, Social Gathering
6	Tue	• House Cleaning, Crack Refilling
7	Wed	• Worship, Travelling
8	Thu	★ Wedding, Moving, Hair Cutting, House Cleaning, Animal Acquiring, Door Fixing, Burial, Travelling
9	Fri	• Hair Cutting, House Cleaning, Bathing, Burial
10	Sat	• Crack Refilling, Animal Acquiring, Planting

★ Lucky Day   • Ordinary Day   ◆ Unlucky Day

Lucky Hours	Direction of Happiness	Direction of Wealth	Direction of Opportunity
03-05 07-09 13-15 17-19 21-23	NE	SE	SW
15-17 17-19 19-21	NW	SE	N
09-11 11-13 15-17 17-19 19-21 21-23	SW	W	NW
09-11 11-13 13-15 17-19 21-23	S	W	NW
01-03 07-09 09-11 13-15 15-17	SE	N	SW
07-09 09-11 11-13 13-15 15-17	NE	N	SW
01-03 11-13 13-15 15-17	NW	E	SW

Monkey – Be careful, you must watch out for money traps. *Rabbit* – It's never too late to correct your mistakes. *Mouse* – God helps those who help themselves. *Horse* – You have to use different tactics to deal with different kinds of clients. *Pig* – Faith moves mountains. *Rooster* – Every cloud has its silver lining.

Date	Day	Favourable Activities
Aug 11	Sun	◆ Unlucky Day Not suitable for important activities
12	Mon	◆ Unlucky Day Not suitable for important activities
13	Tue	★ Construction, Animal Acquiring, Planting, Capturing, Blessing, Travelling, Burial
14	Wed	◆ Unlucky Day Not suitable for important activities
15	Thu	• Worship, Burial
16	Fri	• Start Learning, Engagement, Worship
17	Sat	★ Signing Contracts, Trading, Engagement, Moving, Grand Opening, Wedding

★ Lucky Day   • Ordinary Day   ◆ Unlucky Day

Lucky Hours			Direction of Happiness	Direction of Wealth	Direction of Opportunity
01-03 05-07 11-13 13-15 19-21			SW	E	S
01-03 05-07 07-09 09-11 13-15			S	S	E
01-03 07-09 09-11 15-17 17-19 19-21			SE	S	E
07-09 13-15 17-19 19-21			NE	SE	NE
05-07 13-15 15-17 19-21 21-23			NW	SE	SW
09-11 15-17 17-19 21-23			SW	W	W
01-03 09-11 11-13 13-15 17-19 19-21			S	W	W

Snake – Faint heart never won fair lady. *Ox* – Try to keep alert to handle the unexpected. *Dog* – Comparisons are odious; try to be content with your present achievements. *Sheep* – A little knowledge is a dangerous thing. *Snake* – Do right and fear no man. *Tiger* – You will have a very romantic period of time with your loved one.

Date	Day	Favourable Activities
Aug 18	Sun	★ Start Learning, Blessing, Engagement, Construction, Moving, Grand Opening, Ditching, Wedding
19	Mon	• Construction
20	Tue	★ Travelling, Door Fixing, Bathing, Animal Acquiring, Money Collecting, House Cleaning
21	Wed	• Bathing, House Cleaning, Hair Cutting, Burial
22	Thu	★ Planting, Animal Acquiring, Construction, Moving, Net Weaving, Grand Opening, Wedding, Burial
23	Fri	• Bathing, Worship, Wall Decorating, Passage Fixing
24	Sat	◆ Unlucky Day Not suitable for important activities

★ Lucky Day   • Ordinary Day   ◆ Unlucky Day

Lucky Hours	Direction of Happiness	Direction of Wealth	Direction of Opportunity
05-07 09-11 13-15 15-17 17-19	SE	N	SW
05-07 09-11 11-13 13-15 15-17	NE	N	SW
01-03 07-09 09-11 11-13 13-15 15-17	NW	E	SW
07-09 09-11 11-13	SW	E	NE
05-07 09-11 13-15 19-21 21-23	S	S	E
05-07 07-09 11-13 19-21 21-23	SE	S	E
01-03 07-09 13-15 15-17	NE	SE	NE

Mouse – Better save more money for a rainy day. *Pig* – It's time to make an objective self-evaluation. *Monkey* – You will have a very good chance to meet someone attractive. *Rabbit* – Concentrate only on important projects. *Horse* – Pay more attention to home safety at the weekend.

Date	Day	Favourable Activities
Aug 25	Sun	• Capturing, Animal Acquiring
26	Mon	◆ Unlucky Day Not suitable for important activities
27	Tue	★ Travelling, Signing Contracts, Trading, Bed Set-up, Engagement, Grand Opening, Wedding, Burial
28	Wed	★ Start Learning, Trading, Animal Acquiring, Construction, Grand Opening, Social Gathering, Burial
29	Thu	★ Signing Contracts, Planting, Animal Acquiring, Construction, Moving, Grand Opening, Wedding
30	Fri	• Start Learning, Construction, Worship, Ditching
31	Sat	• Travelling, Construction, Worship, Wall Decorating

★ Lucky Day   • Ordinary Day   ◆ Unlucky Day

Lucky Hours	Direction of Happiness	Direction of Wealth	Direction of Opportunity
01-03 05-07 15-17 17-19	NW	SE	N
05-07 11-13 17-19	SW	W	W
11-13 13-15	S	W	NW
01-03 05-07 09-11 13-15 15-17 17-19	SE	N	NE
11-13 13-15 15-17	NE	N	SW
01-03 11-13 13-15 15-17 17-19	NW	E	SW
05-07 09-11 11-13 15-17	SW	E	S

Rooster – When things are at their worst, they begin to mend. *Tiger* – It's worth giving up your pride to save your love. *Dog* – Watch your safety carefully during outdoor activities. *Dragon* – Business before pleasure. *Sheep* – Better follow the advice of experts in business planning and investments.

Date	Day	Favourable Activities
Sep 1	Sun	★ Travelling Stove Set-up, Engagement, Moving, Grand Opening, Wedding, Social Gathering, Burial
2	Mon	★ Tailoring, House Cleaning, Construction, Animal Acquiring, Planting, Burial
3	Tue	★ Crack Refilling, Social Gathering, Hair Cutting, Money Collecting, Planting
4	Wed	• Bathing, Worship, Wall Decorating, Passage Fixing
5	Thu	◆ Unlucky Day Not suitable for important activities
6	Fri	★ Travelling, Engagement, Planting, Animal Acquiring, Construction, Wedding, Social Gathering, Burial
7	Sat	◆ Unlucky Day Not suitable for important activities

★ Lucky Day   • Ordinary Day   ◆ Unlucky Day

Lucky Hours			Direction of Happiness	Direction of Wealth	Direction of Opportunity
01-03	05-07	07-09	S	S	E
09-11	13-15	17-19			
01-03	07-09	09-11	SE	S	SE
15-17					
01-03	05-07	09-11	NE	SE	NE
13-15					
01-03	05-07	13-15	NW	SE	SW
01-03	09-11	17-19	SW	W	W
19-21	21-23				
09-11	11-13	17-19	S	W	NW
21-23					
01-03	07-09	09-11	SE	N	NE
11-13	13-15				

Ox – The more you work, the more you get. *Pig* – Try to keep a tight budget to avoid money troubles. *Dog* – Watch your diet carefully to avoid food poisoning. *Snake* – Don't play tricks or you will surely be punished. *Horse* – Be more considerate to others if you don't want to be isolated.

Date	Day	Favourable Activities
Sep 8	Sun	◆ Unlucky Day Not suitable for important activities
9	Mon	★ Wedding, Grand Opening, Moving, Blessing, Bed Set-up, Trading, Travelling, Burial
10	Tue	★ Grand Opening, Moving, Worship, Construction, Engagement, Trading, Travelling, Start Learning
11	Wed	● Worship, Capturing
12	Thu	★ Social Gathering, Wedding, Animal Acquiring, Engagement, Blessing, Travelling, Start Learning
13	Fri	★ Tailoring, Hair Cutting, Planting, Burial
14	Sat	● House Cleaning, Bathing

★ Lucky Day   ● Ordinary Day   ◆ Unlucky Day

Lucky Hours	Direction of Happiness	Direction of Wealth	Direction of Opportunity
03-05 11-13 13-15	NE	N	SW
01-03 03-05 07-09 09-11 11-13 13-15 21-23	NW	E	NE
01-03 03-05 09-11 11-13 13-15 19-21	SW	E	NE
01-03 03-05 09-11 13-15 19-21	S	S	E
03-05 09-11 11-13 19-21	SE	S	E
01-03 07-09 09-11 13-15 15-17 17-19	NE	SE	SW
01-03 03-05 07-09 15-17 17-19	NW	SE	SW

Mouse – Don't rush, or your careless mistakes will be costly at this stage. *Monkey* – Don't try to copy other people's ideas. *Rabbit* – Empty vessels make the most sound. *Rooster* – Try to pick up your momentum at work again. *Dragon* – Try not to mix your personal life with your business.

Date	Day	Favourable Activities
Sep 15	Sun	• Hair Cutting, House Cleaning, Planting, Travelling
16	Mon	★ Travelling, Signing Contracts, Trading, Money Collecting, Moving, Grand Opening
17	Tue	◆ Unlucky Day Not suitable for important activities
18	Wed	★ Social Gathering, Wedding, Construction, Engagement, Trading, Signing Contracts
19	Thu	• Burial, Bathing, Capturing, Hair Cutting
20	Fri	◆ Unlucky Day Not suitable for important activities
21	Sat	• Blessing, Worship, Tailoring

★ Lucky Day   • Ordinary Day   ◆ Unlucky Day

Lucky Hours	Direction of Happiness	Direction of Wealth	Direction of Opportunity
03-05 09-11 15-17 17-19 19-21 21-23	SW	W	W
01-03 03-05 11-13 13-15 17-19 19-21 21-23	S	W	W
01-03 07-09 09-11 15-17 17-19	SE	N	NE
03-05 09-11 15-17 17-19	NE	N	N
01-03 03-05 07-09	NW	E	NE
03-05 09-11 11-13 19-21	SW	E	NE
01-03 03-05 09-11 17-19 21-23	S	S	E

Sheep – Keep away from raw food and seafood. *Dog* – Lock your windows and doors to avoid a burglary. *Tiger* – If possible, try to take a vacation to refresh yourself. *Snake* – He that would eat the fruit must climb the tree. *Ox* – Don't try your luck at gambling. *Dog* – Try to keep a low profile to avoid jealousy.

Date	Day	Favourable Activities
Sep 22	Sun	★ Social Gathering, Wedding, Grand Opening, Moving, Construction, Engagement, Travelling, Start Learning
23	Mon	• Capturing, Worship
24	Tue	★ Start Learning, Travelling, Money Collecting, Moving, Tailoring, Grand Opening, Wedding, Social Gathering
25	Wed	• Tailoring, Worship, Hair Cutting, Bathing
26	Thu	★ Worship, Hair Cutting, House Cleaning, Bathing, Burial
27	Fri	★ Travelling, Planting, Construction, House Cleaning, Hair Cutting, Worship
28	Sat	★ Travelling, Signing Contracts, Trading, Blessing, Moving, Net Weaving, Grand Opening, Social Gathering

★ Lucky Day   • Ordinary Day   ◆ Unlucky Day

Lucky Hours			Direction of Happiness	Direction of Wealth	Direction of Opportunity
07-09 09-11 15-17 19-21			SE	S	SE
01-03 03-05 13-15 17-19			NE	SE	SW
03-05 15-17 19-21 21-23			NW	SE	SW
01-03 09-11 13-15 15-17 17-19 19-21 21-23			SW	W	W
01-03 11-13 13-15 17-19 21-23			S	W	NW
01-03 11-13 13-15 15-17			SE	N	NE
03-05 11-13 13-15 15-17			NE	N	SW

Horse – Try to be money-wise or you will lose a lot of cash. *Rabbit* – Don't fool around with your business. *Mouse* – Honesty is the best policy. *Rooster* – Keep a keen eye; you can't judge a book by its cover. *Dragon* – Hope for the best and prepare for the worst. *Monkey* – Try to make good use of your imagination.

Date	Day	Favourable Activities
Sep 29	Sun	◆ Unlucky Day Not suitable for important activities
30	Mon	★ Social Gathering, Tailoring, Net Weaving, Money Collecting, Door Fixing
Oct 1	Tue	● Net Weaving, Capturing, Door Fixing, Stove Set-up
2	Wed	◆ Unlucky Day Not suitable for important activities
3	Thu	● Worship, Capturing, Hunting, Bed Set-up
4	Fri	★ Start Learning, Signing Contracts, Trading, Blessing, Construction, Moving, Grand Opening, Wedding
5	Sat	● Capturing, Worship

★ Lucky Day   ● Ordinary Day   ◆ Unlucky Day

Lucky Hours			Direction of Happiness	Direction of Wealth	Direction of Opportunity
01-03 13-15 15-17 17-19			NW	E	NE
01-03 03-05 09-11 11-13 15-17 21-23			SW	E	NE
01-03 03-05 13-15 19-21			S	S	E
03-05 19-21			SE	S	E
01-03 03-05 07-09 13-15 17-19 21-23			NE	SE	SW
01-03 15-17 17-19 19-21			NW	SE	N
09-11 11-13 15-17 17-19 19-21 21-23			SW	W	NW

Snake – Don't be afraid to take a calculated risk. *Dog* – Take things step by step at works to avoid a sudden big fall. *Ox* – Be gentle and kind to the children around you. *Sheep* – Try to be more flexible in your career. *Tiger* – Keep alert; many unexpected things will happen. *Pig* – Calm your emotions or your friends will be scared away.

Date	Day	Favourable Activities
Oct 6	Sun	★ Start Learning, Travelling, Animal Acquiring, Worship, Moving, Tailoring
7	Mon	★ Bathing, Planting, House Cleaning, Hair Cutting, Burial
8	Tue	• Worship
9	Wed	★ Tailoring, Moving, Worship, Travelling, Money Collecting, Animal Acquiring
10	Thu	◆ Unlucky Day Not suitable for important activities
11	Fri	◆ Unlucky Day Not suitable for important activities
12	Sat	• Passage Fixing

★ Lucky Day   • Ordinary Day   ◆ Unlucky Day

Lucky Hours			Direction of Happiness	Direction of Wealth	Direction of Opportunity
09-11 11-13 13-15 17-19 21-23			S	W	NW
01-03 07-09 09-11 13-15 15-17			SE	N	SW
07-09 09-11 11-13 13-15 15-17			NE	N	SW
01-03 11-13 13-15 15-17			NW	E	SW
01-03 03-05 05-07 11-13 13-15 19-21			SW	E	S
01-03 03-05 05-07 09-11 13-15			S	S	E
01-03 09-11 15-17 17-19 19-21			SE	S	E

Mouse – Better try to adjust to your new environment as soon as possible. *Dragon* – Don't get mad, get even. *Rooster* – Don't show off too much in either your business or private life. *Rabbit* – A compromise at this stage will save a lot of trouble. *Horse* – Watch out, try not to be eaten by big fish in business.

Date	Day	Favourable Activities
Oct 13	Sun	• Burial
14	Mon	• Door Fixing, Bed Set-up, Bathing, Worship
15	Tue	◆ Unlucky Day Not suitable for important activities
16	Wed	• Bed Set-up, Hunting, Animal Acquiring, Worship
17	Thu	★ Travelling, Trading, Engagement, Animal Acquiring, Construction, Moving, Grand Opening, Wedding
18	Fri	• Hunting, Capturing
19	Sat	★ Start Learning, Travelling, Blessing, Moving, Grand Opening, Ditching, Nursery Set-up

★ Lucky Day   • Ordinary Day   ◆ Unlucky Day

Lucky Hours			Direction of Happiness	Direction of Wealth	Direction of Opportunity
03-05	13-15	17-19	NE	SE	NE
19-21					
03-05	05-07	13-15	NW	SE	SW
15-17	19-21	21-23			
09-11	15-17	17-19	SW	W	W
21-23					
01-03	09-11	11-13	S	W	W
13-15	17-19	19-21			
05-07	13-15	15-17	SE	N	SW
17-19					
03-05	05-07	09-11	NE	N	SW
11-13	13-15	15-17			
01-03	09-11	11-13	NW	E	SW
13-15	15-17				

Monkey – Don't be too hesitant, or you will be very sorry later on. *Pig* – Unity is strength, so try not to be isolated. *Tiger* – Laugh and the world laughs with you. *Ox* – Watch your safety closely when you go swimming or fishing. *Dog* – Make a good choice, because only good seeds make a good crop

Date	Day	Favourable Activities
Oct 20	Sun	• Bathing, House Cleaning, Hair Cutting, Tailoring
21	Mon	★ Travelling, Engagement, Moving, Animal Acquiring, Social Gathering
22	Tue	• Stove Set-up, Bathing, House Cleaning, Worship
23	Wed	◆ Unlucky Day Not suitable for important activities
24	Thu	• Wall Decorating, Passage Fixing
25	Fri	• Construction, Burial
26	Sat	★ Construction, Worship, Wedding, Social Gathering, Burial

★ Lucky Day   • Ordinary Day   ◆ Unlucky Day

Lucky Hours			Direction of Happiness	Direction of Wealth	Direction of Opportunity
03-05	09-11	11-13	SW	E	NE
03-05 05-07 09-11 13-15 19-21 21-23			S	S	E
03-05 05-07 11-13 19-21 21-23			SE	S	E
01-03 03-05 13-15 15-17			NE	SE	NE
01-03 03-05 05-07 15-17 17-19			NW	SE	N
05-07	11-13	17-19	SW	W	W
03-05	11-13	13-15	S	W	NW

Dragon – Don't let greed blind you. *Ox* – Forget about gambling if you don't want to have money problems. *Sheep* – A carpenter is known by his chips. *Rooster* – Keep your mouth shut and your eyes wide open. *Rabbit* – A bad schedule will spoil everything. *Horse* – Try to improve your business skills.

Date	Day	Favourable Activities
Oct 27	Sun	◆ Unlucky Day Not suitable for important activities
28	Mon	● Bed Set-up, Hunting, Worship, Net Weaving
29	Tue	★ Travelling, Trading, Engagement, Construction, Moving, Grand Opening, Wedding, Burial
30	Wed	● Worship, Capturing
31	Thu	★ Start Learning, Travelling, Blessing, Planting, Money Collecting, Construction, Moving, Grand Opening
Nov 1	Fri	★ Bathing, House Cleaning, Worship, Hair Cutting, Crack Refilling
2	Sat	● Worship

★ Lucky Day   ● Ordinary Day   ◆ Unlucky Day

Lucky Hours			Direction of Happiness	Direction of Wealth	Direction of Opportunity
01-03	05-07	09-11	SE	N	NE
13-15	15-17	17-19			
03-05	11-13	13-15	NE	N	SW
15-17					
01-03	03-05	11-13	NW	E	SW
13-15	15-17	17-19			
03-05	05-07	09-11	SW	E	S
11-13	15-17				
01-03	05-07	09-11	S	S	E
13-15	17-19				
01-03	03-05	09-11	SE	S	SE
15-17					
01-03	03-05	05-07	NE	SE	NE
09-11	13-15				

Mouse – Keep away from dangerous heights. *Dog* – Better to consult your friends before you make any decisions in love affairs. *Tiger* – Mind your tongue at social gatherings. *Snake* – It is easier to pull down than to put up. *Monkey* – Watch the safety and health of elderly family members.

Date	Day	Favourable Activities
Nov 3	Sun	★ Social Gathering, Hair Cutting, House Cleaning, Bathing, Door Fixing, Stove Set-up
4	Mon	◆ Unlucky Day Not suitable for important activities
5	Tue	• Crack Refilling
6	Wed	• Net Weaving, Fishing
7	Thu	★ Social Gathering, Wedding, Worship, Construction, Animal Acquiring, Capturing, Burial
8	Fri	★ Engagement, Animal Acquiring, Hair Cutting, Worship, Moving, Tailoring, Wedding, Burial
9	Sat	◆ Unlucky Day Not suitable for important activities

★ Lucky Day   • Ordinary Day   ◆ Unlucky Day

Lucky Hours	Direction of Happiness	Direction of Wealth	Direction of Opportunity
01-03 03-05 05-07 13-15	NW	SE	SW
01-03 09-11 17-19 19-21 21-23	SW	W	W
09-11 11-13 17-19 21-23	S	W	NW
01-03 05-07 09-11 11-13 13-15	SE	N	NE
03-05 05-07 11-13 13-15	NE	N	SW
01-03 03-05 07-09 11-13 13-15 21-23	NW	E	NE
01-03 03-05 11-13 13-15 19-21	SW	E	NE

Pig – It will be profitable for you to sell property or valuables. *Dragon* – Forgiveness in your private life will bring you a nice surprise. *Rooster* – Don't exhaust yourself with a heavy workload. *Horse* – Let bygones be bygones. *Sheep* – Don't go near the water. *Ox* – Try to find a good partner for your future development.

Date	Day	Favourable Activities
Nov 10	Sun	• Hunting, Worship, Tailoring
11	Mon	★ Start Learning, Trading, Bed Set-up, Engagement, Construction, Grand Opening
12	Tue	★ Start Learning, Travelling, Planting, Construction, Moving, Wedding, Social Gathering, Burial
13	Wed	★ Start Learning, Travelling, Wedding, Animal Acquiring, Construction, Hair Cutting, Tailoring, Nursery Set-up
14	Thu	• Tailoring, Net Weaving
15	Fri	• Bathing, Worship
16	Sat	◆ Unlucky Day Not suitable for important activities

★ Lucky Day   • Ordinary Day   ◆ Unlucky Day

Lucky Hours			Direction of Happiness	Direction of Wealth	Direction of Opportunity
01-03 03-05 05-07 13-15 21-23			S	S	E
03-05 05-07 11-13 19-21			SE	S	E
01-03 07-09 13-15 15-17 17-19			NE	SE	SW
01-03 03-05 15-17 17-19			NW	SE	SW
05-07 07-09 15-17 17-19 19-21 21-23			SW	W	W
01-03 03-05 11-13 13-15 17-19 19-21 21-23			S	W	W
01-03 05-07 07-09 15-17 17-19			SE	N	NE

Rabbit – You never miss the water until the well runs dry. *Dog* – Don't be too greedy about money, or you will be easily cheated. *Mouse* – Bad money will drive out good. *Tiger* – Try not to challenge or provoke your superiors. *Monkey* – Try to cheer up your co-workers. *Snake* – Not a good time for investments.

Date	Day	Favourable Activities
Nov 17	Sun	• Worship, Social Gathering, Crack Refilling
18	Mon	★ Travelling, Trading, Engagement, Construction, Moving, Grand Opening, Wedding, Burial
19	Tue	★ Travelling, Signing Contracts, Trading, Engagement, Construction, Moving, Grand Opening, Wedding
20	Wed	• Hunting, Capturing, Hair Cutting, Net Weaving
21	Thu	◆ Unlucky Day Not suitable for important activities
22	Fri	★ Travelling, Bed Set-up, Engagement, Construction, Moving, Wedding, Social Gathering, Burial
23	Sat	★ Start Learning, Signing Contracts, Trading, Door Fixing, Construction, Grand Opening, Burial

★ Lucky Day   • Ordinary Day   ◆ Unlucky Day

Lucky Hours			Direction of Happiness	Direction of Wealth	Direction of Opportunity
03-05	05-07	15-17 17-19	NE	N	N
01-03	03-05	05-07 07-09	NW	E	NE
03-05	05-07	11-13 19-21	SW	E	NE
01-03	03-05	05-07 17-19 21-23	S	S	E
05-07	07-09	15-17 19-21	SE	S	SE
01-03	03-05	13-15 17-19	NE	SE	SW
03-05	05-07	15-17 19-21 21-23	NW	SE	SW

Pig – Try to keep your business secrets a secret, and never talk about them in public. *Dragon* – A bird in the hand is worth two in the bush. *Ox* – Try to lighten your heart. *Horse* – You will see good profits from your investments. *Rooster* – Business before pleasure. *Sheep* – Walk and drive with extreme care.

Date	Day	Favourable Activities
Nov 24	Sun	• Hunting, Capturing, House Cleaning
25	Mon	★ Start Learning, Bed Set-up, Bathing, Construction, House Cleaning, Worship
26	Tue	• Construction
27	Wed	• Worship, Social Gathering
28	Thu	◆ Unlucky Day Not suitable for important activities
29	Fri	• Hair Cutting, Social Gathering, Crack Refilling
30	Sat	★ Travelling, Trading, Engagement, Planting, Construction, Moving, Grand Opening, Wedding

★ Lucky Day   • Ordinary Day   ◆ Unlucky Day

Lucky Hours			Direction of Happiness	Direction of Wealth	Direction of Opportunity
01-03	13-15	15-17	SW	W	W
17-19	19-21	21-23			
01-03	11-13	13-15	S	W	NW
17-19	21-23				
01-03	05-07	11-13	SE	N	NE
13-15	15-17				
03-05	05-07	11-13	NE	N	SW
13-15	15-17				
01-03	13-15	15-17	NW	E	NE
17-19					
01-03	03-05	05-07	SW	E	NE
11-13	15-17	21-23			
01-03	03-05	05-07	S	S	E
13-15	19-21				

Rabbit – Try to get the necessary support of co-workers. *Mouse* – Watch your step to make sure that you don't fall into traps. *Monkey* – Think positively and try not to give up. *Snake* – Keep your eyes wide open to possible trouble. *Dog* – Don't be too greedy; enough is as good as a feast.

Date	Day	Favourable Activities
Dec 1	Sun	★ Travelling, Engagement, Moving, Money Collecting, Construction, Net Weaving, Grand Opening, Wedding
2	Mon	★ Blessing, Capturing, Moving, Animal Acquiring, Tailoring, Wedding, Social Gathering, Burial
3	Tue	◆ Unlucky Day Not suitable for important activities
4	Wed	◆ Unlucky Day Not suitable for important activities
5	Thu	★ Start Learning, Signing Contracts, Trading, Animal Acquiring, Construction, Tailoring, Grand Opening, Social Gathering
6	Fri	● Bathing, Capturing, House Cleaning
7	Sat	◆ Start Learning, Travelling, Construction, Moving, Tailoring, Grand Opening, Wedding, Nursery, Set-up

★ Lucky Day   ● Ordinary Day   ◆ Unlucky Day

Lucky Hours			Direction of Happiness	Direction of Wealth	Direction of Opportunity
03-05	05-07	19-21	SE	S	E
01-03 03-05 07-09 13-15 17-19 21-23			NE	SE	SW
01-03 15-17 17-19 19-21			NW	SE	N
11-13 15-17 17-19 19-21 21-23			SW	W .	NW
11-13 13-15 17-19 21-23			S	W	NW
01-03 07-09 13-15 15-17			SE	N	SW
07-09 11-13 13-15 15-17			NE	N	SW

Tiger – Take care of yourself to avoid a bad cold. *Dragon* – Set a target according to your abilities. *Ox* – Go ahead, you will be able to overcome most at work. *Pig* – Better check the leaks in your present accounting systems. *Sheep* – Try to keep your promises; your actions will speak louder than words.

Date	Day	Favourable Activities
Dec 8	Sun	★ Start Learning, Blessing, Planting, Construction, Ditching, Nursery Set-up
9	Mon	◆ Unlucky Day Not suitable for important activities
10	Tue	◆ Unlucky Day Not suitable for important activities
11	Wed	★ Travelling, Trading, Construction, Hair Cutting, Moving, Grand Opening, Wedding
12	Thu	★ Grand Opening, Net Weaving, Construction, Money Collecting, Planting, Trading, Signing Contracts, Travelling
13	Fri	• Wall Decorating, Passage Fixing
14	Sat	★ Wedding, Tailoring, Net Weaving, Construction, Engagement, Door Fixing, Trading

★ Lucky Day   • Ordinary Day   ◆ Unlucky Day

Lucky Hours			Direction of Happiness	Direction of Wealth	Direction of Opportunity
01-03	13-15	15-17	NW	E	SW
01-03 03-05 05-07 13-15 19-21			SW	E	S
01-03 03-05 05-07 07-09 09-11 13-15			S	S	E
01-03 07-09 09-11 15-17 17-19 19-21			SE	S	E
03-05 07-09 13-15 17-19 19-21			NE	SE	NE
03-05 05-07 13-15 15-17 19-21 21-23			NW	SE	SW
09-11 15-17 17-19 21-23			SW	W	W

Rooster – What can't be cured must be endured. *Horse* – Try to mind your own business. *Mouse* – Team work is very important, because a bird never flew on one wing. *Rabbit* – Better try to get as much rest and sleep as possible to avoid a sudden collapse. *Snake* – Try to be more friendly to new acquaintances.

Date	Day	Favourable Activities
Dec 15	Sun	• Capturing, Worship
16	Mon	◆ Unlucky Day Not suitable for important activities
17	Tue	• Fishing, Hair Cutting
18	Wed	★ Start Learning, Travelling, Trading, House Cleaning, Moving, Grand Opening, Burial
19	Thu	• Hunting, House Cleaning, Hair Cutting, Tailoring
20	Fri	★ Start Learning, Blessing, Engagement, Construction, Grand Opening, Nursery Set-up
21	Sat	• Bathing, Crack Refilling

★ Lucky Day   • Ordinary Day   ◆ Unlucky Day

Lucky Hours			Direction of Happiness	Direction of Wealth	Direction of Opportunity
01-03 09-11 13-15 17-19 19-21			S	W	W
05-07 09-11 13-15 15-17 17-19			SE	N	SW
03-05 05-07 09-11 13-15 15-17			NE	N	SW
01-03 07-09 09-11 13-15 15-17			NW	E	SW
03-05 07-09 09-11			SW	E	NE
03-05 05-07 09-11 13-15 19-21 21-23			S	S	E
03-05 05-07 07-09 19-21 21-23			SE	S	E

Dog – Try harder; hard work breaks no bones. *Monkey* – Try to take care of a very delicate relationship with your loved ones. *Ox* – The early bird catches the worm. *Tiger* – Not a good time for carrying out new projects. *Dragon* – One good turn deserves another. *Pig* – Hurry up, because time and tide wait for no man.

Date	Day	Favourable Activities
Dec 22	Sun	◆ Unlucky Day Not suitable for important activities
23	Mon	★ Travelling, Trading, Blessing, Construction, Moving, Wedding, Social Gathering, Burial
24	Tue	★ Travelling, Signing Contracts, Trading, Planting, Construction, Tailoring, Grand Opening, Social Gathering
25	Wed	• Wall Decorating, Passage Fixing
26	Thu	★ Signing Contracts, Trading, Blessing, Engagement, Animal Acquiring, Construction, Wedding
27	Fri	• Hunting, Capturing, Worship, Nursery Set-up
28	Sat	◆ Unlucky Day Not suitable for important activities

★ Lucky Day   • Ordinary Day   ◆ Unlucky Day

Lucky Hours	Direction of Happiness	Direction of Wealth	Direction of Opportunity
01-03 03-05 07-09 13-15 15-17	NE	SE	NE
01-03 03-05 05-07 15-17 17-19	NW	SE	N
05-07 17-19	SW	W	W
03-05 13-15	S	W	NW
01-03 05-07 09-11 13-15 15-17 17-19	SE	N	NE
03-05 13-15 15-17	NE	N	SW
01-03 03-05 13-15 15-17 17-19	NW	E	SW

Horse – Ask no questions and hear no lies. *Mouse* – You'd better try to keep away from wicked so-called friends. *Rooster* – Forget about your previous losses and concentrate only on current projects. *Snake* – Don't indulge yourself too much in sex and alcohol. *Sheep* – It's time to take a vacation to refresh yourself.

Date	Day	Favourable Activities
Dec 29	Sun	• Hunting, Net Weaving
30	Mon	★ Start Learning, Travelling, Trading, Moving, Grand Opening, Wedding, Social Gathering, Burial
31	Tue	• Bathing, Capturing, House Cleaning, Hair Cutting

★ Lucky Day   • Ordinary Day   ◆ Unlucky Day

Lucky Hours	Direction of Happiness	Direction of Wealth	Direction of Opportunity
03-05 05-07 09-11 15-17	SW	E	S
01-03 05-07 07-09 09-11 13-15 17-19	S	S	E
01-03 03-05 07-09 09-11 15-17	SE	S	SE

Snake – Keep your mouth shut, because the walls have ears. *Dog* – Save more money for unexpected expenses. *Pig* – You will have some luck at lotteries and gambling. *Ox* – You will have a romantic weekend with your loved one. *Dragon* – Don't eat raw food or seafood. *Tiger* – Watch out closely for the danger of fire at home.

Chinese Success Signs

Neil Somerville

A fascinating and comprehensive look at Chinese Horoscopes that shows how you can tap into the hidden potential of your Chinese Success Sign.

Read this book and discover:

- Your sign and its associated strengths and weaknesses
- What work suits your best
- How you relate to others and how to get on best with each sign
- How you fare in love and romance
- Your attitude to money, plus tips to help you develop your money making abilities
- The distinct life phases of your sign and how to make the best of them
- The secrets of successful people born under your sign
- How you can realize your true potential

Your Chinese Horoscope for 2002

What the year of the horse holds in store for you

Neil Somerville

The Year 2002 is the Chinese Year of the Horse – what will this mean for you? This complete guide contains all the predictions you need to take you through the year.

Chinese Astrology is being rediscovered in the West and is proving to be a highly accurate system of character analysis and prediction. This best-selling guide – now in its 15th year – includes:

- Everything you need to know about the 12 signs of the Chinese zodiac
- An explanation of the Five Elements, and which one governs your sign
- Individual predictions to help you find love, luck and success